These sermons were preached by a man who, many believe, had the greatest healing ministry of his time, first as a missionary to South Africa, and later in Spokane, Washington, where 100,000 healings were recorded in five years.

DR. JOHN G. LAKE

The John G. Lake Sermons

on Dominion over Demons,
Disease and Death

A series of faith-inspiring messages by Dr. John G.
Lake whose healing ministry in missionary fields was
considered the greatest of his generation.

Edited by
Gordon Lindsay

Published by
CHRIST FOR THE NATIONS INC.
Dallas, Texas
Reprint 2002

Cover design by Virginia Sanz.

INDEX OF CHAPTERS

FOREWORD

The sermons in this volume were preached by Dr. John G. Lake during the height of his ministry. There is a special reason that I have a very personal interest in them. Early in my preaching career, as I lay apparently dying from ptomaine poisoning, a number of these sermons in typewritten form were brought to me. I had just strength enough to read a few pages at a time. The powerful truths contained in these sermons slowly sank into my consciousness. Then they came to me with great force. Suddenly I arose from my bed, and instead of dying I found that I was a well man.

Now for the first time, with two or three exceptions, those sermons appear in print, and I trust that they will be an equal blessing to the many who read them. In making these messages available to the public, I trust that in some measure I have discharged an obligation which I have owed Dr. Lake for the rich legacy of faith that his ministry brought to my soul, during my formative years. Also to his dear wife, Florence Lake, who assisted in my care during the above-mentioned serious illness.

September 20, 1949
Box 4097
Shreveport, La.

CONSECRATION PRAYER

My God and Father, in Jesus' Name I come to thee. Take me as I am. Make me what I ought to be in spirit, in soul, and body. Give me power to do right; if I have wronged any, to repent, to confess, to restore, no matter what it costs. Wash me in the Blood of Jesus, that I may become thy child, and manifest thee in a perfect spirit, a holy mind, a sickless body, to the glory of God. Amen.

Chapter I

HOW GOD GAVE ME THE MINISTRY OF HEALING AND SENT ME TO AFRICA

Eight years passed after God revealed Jesus the Healer to me. I had been practicing the ministry of healing. During that eight years every answer to prayer, every miraculous touch of God, every response of my own soul to the Spirit had created within me a more intense longing for an intimacy and a consciousness of God, like I felt the disciples of Jesus and the primitive church had possessed.

He Receives Special Anointing of the Spirit

Shortly after my entrance into the ministry of healing, while attending a service where the necessity for the Baptism of the Spirit was presented, as I knelt in prayer and reconsecration to God, an anointing of the Spirit came upon me. Waves of Holy Glory passed through my being, and I was lifted into a new realm of God's presence and power. After this, answers to prayer were frequent and miracles of healing occurred from time to time. I felt myself on the borderland of a great spiritual realm, but was unable to enter in fully, so my nature was not satisfied with the attainment.

Finally I was led to set aside certain hours of the day that I dedicated to God, as times of meditation and prayer. Thus a number of months passed, until one morning as I knelt praying the Spirit of the Lord spoke within my spirit, and said, "Be patient until autumn." My heart rejoiced in this encouragement and I continued my practice of meditation and prayer as formerly. It became easy for me to detach myself from the course of life, so that while my hands and mind were engaged in the common affairs of every day, my spirit maintained its attitude of communion with God.

5

At this time in addition to my work as minister of the Gospel, I was engaged as a manager of agents for a life insurance company. During the period of which I speak, I preached practically every night. After the services I was in the habit of joining a circle of friends who like myself were determined to pray through into God where we could receive the Baptism of the Holy Ghost, as we believed the early disciples had received it. I said, "God, if you will baptize me in the Holy Spirit, and give me the power of God, nothing shall be permitted to stand between me and a hundred-fold obedience."

He Receives the Baptism of the Holy Ghost

One afternoon a brother minister called and invited me to accompany him to visit a lady who was sick. Arriving at the home we found the lady in a wheel chair. All her joints were set with inflammatory rheumatism. She had been in the condition for ten years.

While my friend was conversing with her, preparing her to be prayed with, that she might be healed, I sat in a deep chair on the opposite side of a large room. My soul was crying out to God in a yearning too deep for words, when suddenly it seemed to me that I had passed under a shower of warm tropical rain, which was not falling upon me but through me. My spirit and soul and body, under this influence, was soothed into such a deep still calm as I had never known. My brain, which had always been so active, became perfectly still. An awe of the presence of God settled over me. I knew it was God.

Some moments passed; I do not know how many. The Spirit said, "I have heard your prayers, I have seen your tears. You are now baptized in the Holy Spirit." Then currents of power began to rush through my being from the crown of my head to the soles of my feet. The shocks of power increased in rapidity and voltage. As these currents of power would pass through me, they seemed to come upon my head, rush through my body and through my feet into the floor. The power was so great that my body began to vibrate intensely so that I believe if I had not been sitting in such a deep low chair I might have fallen upon the floor.

At that moment I observed my friend was motioning me to come and join him in prayer for the woman who was sick. In his absorption he had not noticed that anything had taken place in me. I arose to go to him, but I found my body trembling so violently that I had difficulty in walking across the room, and especially in controlling the trembling of my hands and arms. I knew that it would not be wise to thus lay my hands upon the sick woman as I was likely to jar her. It occurred to me that all that was necessary was to touch the tips of my fingers on the top of the patient's head and then the vibrations would not jar her. This I did. At once the currents of holy power passed through my being, and I knew that it likewise passed through the one that was sick. She did not speak, but apparently was amazed at the effect in her body.

My friend who had been talking to her in his great earnestness had been kneeling as he talked to her. He arose saying, "Let us pray that the Lord will now heal you." As he did so he took her by the hand. At the instant their hands touched, a flash of dynamic power went through my person and through the sick woman, and as my friend held her hand the shock of power went through her hand into him. The rush of power into his person was so great that it caused him to fall on the floor. He looked up at me with joy and surprise, and springing to his feet said, "Praise the Lord, John, Jesus has baptized you in the Holy Ghost!"

Then he took the crippled hand, that had been set for so many years. The clenched hands opened and the joints began to work, first the fingers, then the hand and the wrist, then the elbow and shoulder.

These were the outward manifestations. But Oh! who could describe the thrills of joy inexpressible that were passing through my spirit? Who could comprehend the peace and presence of God that thrilled my soul? Even at this late date, ten years afterward, the awe of that hour rests upon my soul. My experience has truly been as Jesus said: "He shall be within you a well of water, springing up into everlasting life." That never-ceasing fountain has flowed through my spirit, soul and body day and night, bringing salvation and healing and the Baptism of the Spirit in the power of God to multitudes.

The Result of the Holy Spirit Baptism

Shortly after my Baptism in the Holy Spirit, a working of the Spirit commenced in me, that seemed to have for its purpose the revelation of the nature of Jesus Christ to me and in me. Through this tuition and remolding of the Spirit a great tenderness for mankind was to awaken in my soul. I saw mankind through new eyes. They seemed to me as wandering sheep, having strayed far, in the midst of confusion, groping and wandering hither and thither. They had no definite aim and did not seem to understand what the difficulty was, or how to return to God.

The desire to proclaim the message of Christ, and to demonstrate His power to save and bless, grew in my soul, until my life was swayed by this overwhelming passion.

The Call Versus Business Interests

However, my heart was divided. I could not follow successfully the ordinary pursuits of life and business. When a man came into my office, though I knew that twenty or thirty minutes of concentration on the business in hand would possibly net me thousands of dollars, I could not discuss business with him. By a new power of discernment I could see his soul, understand his inner life and motives. I recognized him as one of the wandering sheep, and longed in an overwhelming desire to help him get to God for salvation and find himself.

I determined to discuss the matter with the president of my company. I frankly told him the condition of soul that I found myself in and its cause. He kindly replied: "You have worked hard, Lake. You need a change. Take a vacation for three months, and if you want to preach, preach. But at the end of three months $50,000.00 a year will look like a lot of money to you, and you will have little desire to sacrifice it for the dreams of religious possibilities."

I thanked him, accepted an invitation to join a brother in evangelistic work, and left the office, never to return.

During the three months, I preached every day to large congregations, saw a multitude of people saved from their sins and healed of their diseases, and hundreds of them baptized in the Holy Ghost. At the end of three months, I said to God: "I am through forever with everything in life but the proclamation and demonstration of the Gospel of Jesus Christ."

I disposed of my estate and distributed my funds in a manner I believed to be for the best interests of the Kingdom of God, and made myself wholly dependent upon God for the support of myself and my family, and abandoned myself to the preaching of Jesus.

The Call to Africa

While ministering in a city in Northern Illinois, the chore boy at the hotel where we were stopping was inquiring for someone to assist him in sawing down a large tree. I volunteered to assist him, and while in the act of sawing down the tree, the Spirit of the Lord spoke within my spirit clear and distinct: "Go to Indianapolis. Prepare for a winter campaign. Get a large hall. In the Spring you will go to Africa."

I went to Indianapolis. The Lord directed me in a marvelous way, so that in a few days I had secured a large hall and was conducting services as He directed. About this time the following incident took place, which has had so much to do with the success of my ministry ever since.

He Receives Power to Cast Out Demons

One morning when I came down to breakfast I found my appetite had disappeared. I could not eat. I went about my work as usual. At dinner I had no desire to eat, and no more in the evening. This went on till the third day. But toward the evening of the third day an overwhelming desire to pray took possession of me. I only wanted to be alone to pray. Prayer flowed from my soul like a stream. I could not cease praying. As soon as it was possible to get a place of seclusion I would kneel to pour out my heart to God for hours. Whatever I was doing, that stream of prayer continued flowing from my soul.

On the night of the sixth day of this fast that the Lord had laid on me, while in the act of washing my hands, the Spirit said to me once again, "Go and pray." I turned around and knelt by my bedside. As I knelt praying, the Spirit said, "How long have you been praying to cast out demons?" and I replied, "Lord, a long time." And the Spirit said, "From henceforth thou shalt cast out demons." I arose and praised God.

The Case of the Demon-Possessed Man

The following night at the close of the service a gentleman came to me, and pointing to a large red-letter motto on the wall, which read, "In my name they shall cast out devils," he said: "Do you believe that?" I replied, "I do." He said, "Do not answer hastily, for I have gone around the land seeking for a minister who would tell me he believed that. Many said that they did, but when I questioned them I found they wanted to qualify the statement." I said, "Brother, so far as I know my soul, I believe it with all my heart."

Then he said, "I will tell you why I asked. Two and one-half years ago my brother who was a manager of a large elevator suddenly became violently insane. He was committed to the asylum, and is there today. Somehow he became possessed of an evil spirit. Physicians who have examined him declare that every function of his body and brain are apparently normal, and they cannot account for his insanity." I replied, "Brother, bring him on."

On Sunday in the midst of the service, the man came, attended by the brother, the mother and an attendant of the institution.

I stopped preaching, selected a half dozen persons whom I knew were people who had faith in God to join me in prayer for his deliverance. I stepped from the platform, laid my hands on his head, and in the Name of Jesus Christ, the Son of God, commanded the devil that possessed him to come out of him. The Spirit of God went through my being like a flash of lightning. I knew in my soul that the evil spirit was cast out, and was not surprised when in a moment the man raised his head and spoke intelligently to me. A few days later he was discharged from the institution, returned home a healed man and resumed his former position as manager of a grain elevator.

Thus God verified His word to me, and from that day to this, the power of God has remained upon my soul, and I have seen hundreds of insane people delivered and healed.

Money Comes to Provide Passage to Africa

One day during the following February my preaching partner said to me, "John, how much will it cost to take our party to Johannesburg, South Africa?" I replied, "Two thousand dollars." He said, "If we are going to Africa in the Spring, it is time you and I were praying for the money." I said, "I have been praying for the money ever since New Year. I have not heard from the Lord or anyone else concerning it." He said, "Never mind, let's pray again." A few days later he returned from the post-office and threw out upon the table four $500 drafts saying, "John, there is the answer. Jesus has sent it. We are going to Africa."

We left Indianapolis on the first day of April, 1908, my wife and self and seven children and four others. We had our tickets to Africa but no money for personal expenses en route except $1.50. (At this point in the narrative Dr. Lake relates several remarkable providences of God which supplied their expenses en route.)

Through my knowledge of the immigration laws of South Africa, I knew that before we would be permitted to land, I must show the immigration inspector that I was possessor of at least $125.00. We prayed earnestly over this matter, and about the time we reached the equator a rest came into my soul concerning it. I could pray no more.

About eight or ten days later we arrived in Cape Town harbor, and our ship anchored. The immigration inspector came on board and the passengers lined up at the purser's office to present their money and receive their tickets to land. My wife said, "What are you going to do?" I said, "I am going to line up with the rest. We have obeyed God thus far. It is now up to the Lord. If they send us back we cannot help it."

As I stood in line awaiting my turn, a fellow passenger touched me on the shoulder and indicated to me to step

out of the line, and come over to the ship's rail to speak
with him. He asked some questions, and then drew from
his pocket a traveler's checkbook, and handed me two
money orders aggregating $200.00. I stepped back into
line, presented my orders to the inspector, and received
our tickets to land.

God Provides Them a Home in Africa

Johannesburg is one thousand miles inland from Cape
Town. Throughout the voyage and on the train we
earnestly prayed about the subject of a home. We were
faith missionaries. We had neither a Board nor friends
behind us to furnish money. We were dependent on God.
Many times during the trip to Johannesburg we bowed
our heads and reminded God that when we arrived there,
we would need a home. God blessed and wondrously
answered our prayer.

Upon our arrival at Johannesburg I observed a little
woman bustling up. She said, "You are an American missionary party?" The reply was, "Yes." Addressing me
she said, "How many are there in your family?" I
answered, "My wife, myself and seven children." "O,"
she said, "you are the family. The Lord has sent me
to meet you, and I want to give you a home."

That same afternoon we were living in a furnished
cottage in the suburbs, the property of our beloved bene-
factor, Mrs. C. L. Goodenough, of Johannesburg, who
remains to this day our beloved friend and fellow worker
in the Lord. She is now a resident of Forida and has
visited us in the West.

Chapter II
DOMINION OF A CHRISTIAN

Divine healing is not a new thing; it is as old as the Book. I have chosen today the first chapter of Genesis with emphasis on the 26th verse:

"And God said, let us make man in our own likeness; and let them have dominion over the fish of the sea, and over the fowl of the air, and over the cattle, and over all the earth, and over every creeping thing that creepeth upon the earth."—Gen. 1:26.

I want you to notice the 31st verse of the same chapter. "And God saw everything that He made, and, behold, it was very good." I read that as a reminder of the fact that God made everything good, and there was a time in the history of the human race when there was not a man or a woman with a cancer or a tumor, or tuberculosis, or Bright's disease, or diabetes, or any one of the ten thousand things that afflict mankind in our day. Now, God said to this man and this woman that He presented to the world, "Let them have dominion." Do you know that the word "dominion" is almost a lost word in the Christian's vocabulary?

Dominion Over Sin First

But in the soul of him who truly knows God and has been in touch with the Lord as his Saviour and Healer, his first awareness is a sense of dominion. Dominion over sin is the first thing the Christian soul becomes aware of, and in the truly God-enlightened soul, dominion over sickness likewise. Having been under the rule of sin, and having come into union with God, the dominion of the Spirit of God manifests itself over sin. And freedom, freedom of consciousness from the control and power of sin, is possibly the first vivid and lasting consciousness in the soul.

14

I cannot imagine that when Adam wanted the cows or the sheep he went out with a dog or a club to get them. Living as he did in the place of God where God had the fullness of access to his nature, he had a better control of the cows and the sheep than that. I believe that when he spoke to the cows they came home; that when he wanted the birds he said "Come," and they came.

It is good for man to know and exercise the authority of God. Usually we hear a good deal more about exercising the authority of God over everything else but ourselves. It seems that in these days men have studied about everything outside of themselves to a greater or lesser degree. But it is almost a sadness that men know so little about themselves. It is good to know the qualities that God has put within the mind and nature of men. Indeed the Scriptures enjoin us to exercise control of ourselves. "Taking every thought into captivity to the obedience of Christ." Not a rambling mind, but a mind controlled, a mind directed, a mind fixed on God, a mind with ideals of God's holiness and wholeness of body, soul and spirit established there. A mind whose very structure contains God, and has capacity to obtain, retain and utilize the greatest degree of the living Spirit of the eternal God. Blessed be His Name!

A Sorry Procession

Suppose we could have lined up this whole audience a couple of years ago, and had them pass before this platform. What a sorry procession it would have been. Miss Celia Prentice would have to pass along in steel braces, with one leg two inches shorter than the other, having been that way from birth. When she passes before the platform today, she walks on equal legs, and her feet are the same size and shape. That was not a healing —that was a work of creation, fulfilling the pattern that was in the mind of God, and bringing the structural form of that girl to where God saw "it was good."

Mrs. Shields would have had to pass, a poor, dying, suffering wreck, as she was when she first came in contact with the gospel and the power of God. Mrs. Reed would have had to pass a poor, suffering soul, full of internal cancers. A sad procession. You can go on down the line and take one after another, and that is almost the story of each individual in this great audience.

But bless God, there was a day when there was not one to pass God's platform with a cancer, nobody had a tumor, or any other form of disease. Our first parents were lovely, sweet and good. Every drop of blood in their body was perfect—100 per cent pure. That is the thing that we are trying these days to get men to understand. God is trying to get them to separate themselves unto Him, so that that same pure life of God that came from heaven, and took possession of men's lives, will come again. And its same divine sweetness and heavenly purity will be recognized in us making us sweet and pure and lovely, body, soul and spirit.

The Redeemer and the Remedy

God, seeing that men were in difficulty, and that sin, sickness and death prevailed, in order to save the race from extermination, was compelled to manifest the Redeemer and the redemption. Jesus Christ came to this world as God's divine remedy. He has no other remedy, but the Lord Jesus Christ. God's remedy is a person not a thing.

When Jesus Christ set up His method of healing in the world it was peculiar and distinct. The devil can manifest some other system, or man can evolve some other system and it may have power in a degree. But God has a particular method. Christ used it because it was divinely superior to every other, and would accomplish a result none other could. No man ever lived in the world who ever caused the eyes to grow in a child that had no eyes, or a man that was born blind to see. No man ever created a remedy in the world that would make a girl's leg to grow two inches, after she was 17 years old, and had been born in that condition. God demonstrates the superiority of His system, and of His power, and His divine remedy, in that it will accomplish in man what nothing else will.

Divine Healing Not Something Separate From Salvation

One of the difficulties that God has to remove from the mind of man on the line of healing is this wretched thing that often prevails in the best of Christian circles where healing is taught and practiced—the idea that divine healing is something disassociated or separate from Christ's salvation. It is not. Healing is simply the salvation of Jesus Christ, having its divine action in a man's flesh, the same as it had its divine action in a man's soul, or in the spirit of man. When Christ healed the body, He healed the soul. All man needs to do is to let God come in. His deficient spiritual eyes receive sight, his dormant mind becomes active, and his sick body is healed. I want to fix this thought in your mind. The healing of an individual is God's demonstration to that soul that he has been forgiven of his sins. If he only has sense enough to believe it, he goes forth from the presence of God free in body, free in soul, free in spirit, healed within and healed without.

When James was discussing the subject he put it in this form: "Is there any sick among you? Let him call for the elders of the church; and let them pray over him. Anointing him with oil in the name of the Lord: And the prayer of faith shall save the sick; and *if he have committed sins, they shall be forgiven him.*" Right there,

right then, bless God, when the healing power of Jesus
Christ comes from heaven, and testifies in that man's
soul by healing his body, his sins likewise are forgiven if
he will only believe it.

Now beloved, that is the service that we are trying to
perform. That when we unite and pray the prayer of
faith, with the intelligence that the Word of God reveals
in that holy Book, there will be a divine result of healing
and forgiveness.

Through Sin Sickness Came Into the World

I want to get to you two outstanding facts this afternoon. First, in the beginning God had a perfect man.
Adam and Eve were perfect people. They were not deficient in a single thing. Then man wandered into sin
and degeneracy. There is a vital relationship between
sickness and sin. That without sin in the race—not necessarily the individual, but without sin in the race, there
would be no such thing as sickness now. Does the Word
of God stand up to that? "Through sin death entered into
the world." What is sickness? It is incipient death. I tell
you beloved, that when you come to God for the healing
of your body, it ought to be with a contrite repentance—
"confessing your sins." Not only sins, transgressions, but
SIN. That state of the soul that causes you to transgress.

The condition that I have been discussing with you is
more than a personal condition. It is a racial one. The
whole race is similarly affected. The active principle of
Bright's disease, tuberculosis, and all that class of disease
is the hellish germ in the system that has no right to be
in the blood, and is asking for life and expression. The
fact is, the race has been polluted through sin unto death.
"Dying we die."

The Will of God Is to Save Man From Sin and Its Effects

Jesus spoke some very simple words. When the leper

said to Jesus, "Lord if thou wilt thou canst make me whole," he recognized that Jesus had the power but was not clear about His willingness. I have no objection to your praying that prayer, providing that you are as ignorant as he was of what the Will of God was. But you are not. Jesus said, "I will." The Word of God is calculated to give intelligence as to what the Will of God is. And from Genesis to Revelation it emphasizes one thing, that the Will of God is to extricate the body, soul and spirit of man from sin, and the effects of sin which is disease and death. And when the Will of God is fully wrought in the race, sin and sickness and death will have disappeared. The beginning of immortality is when God breathes His Life into you and me, and our spirits become the recipients of eternal life in Jesus Christ forever.

How simple it should be for the people who have this confidence and faith in the Lord Jesus Christ and His salvation, to add faith for the body as well as the spirit.

One of the most enjoyable freedoms in the world is the mental and spiritual freedom that comes with the escape from the bondage of fear. The fear of sickness. The fear of this difficulty and the fear of that difficulty. Our God says He is the Almighty One. He invites us to have confidence in Him because of His Almightiness. All things are possible to him that believeth. Isn't that a beautiful relationship? A relationship so vital that the Almightiness of God comes into your soul. Why? Because of believing faith. God bless you.

Chapter III

THE VALUE OF A COVENANT WITH GOD

I want to bring you some of the facts of Scripture that bear on the value of a covenant with God. I shall use as my subject Exod. 15:26. God calls His people into a special relationship with Himself. God binds Himself by covenants, and a covenant is more than a contract. A contract is an agreement between two parties. A covenant is more. For instance the State of South Carolina grants no divorce upon this ground. Marriage is not a legal contract in the state of South Carolina. It is a covenant. They explain a covenant like this. A man and woman have covenanted with Almighty God to live together as man and wife. At a later time the man and woman may change their minds, but the law holds that God, being a party to that covenant, does not change His mind. He is the first party, the man and the woman the second party. One party alone cannot break the agreement. The covenant must be dissolved by both parties.

God Is a Party in the Covenant of Healing

Beloved, I want you to see that God is a party in the Covenant of Healing. It is an eternal arrangement, eternally binding. God entered into covenant with man when the Children of Israel were formed into a nation after their escape from the land of Egypt. He made the arrangements for the acceptance of other people who were not Israelites to be received into the nation under certain conditions. The party thus wanting to be related to Israel and become a part of it, would have to subscribe to the terms of the original covenant God made with Abraham. Exod. 12:48-49.

We find instances in which there was a violation of

a covenant, and we notice the far-reaching consequences. The sons of Jacob covenanted with the Shechemites to give their sister to the prince, Shechem, in marriage. The covenant was sealed by the rite of circumcision. But instead of adhering to the covenant, Levi and Simeon in the anger of their soul took their swords and slew all the males in the city of Shechem and robbed them of their possessions. The result of this act was to bring the brothers under the judgment of God. Old Jacob prophecying in the Spirit, spake, "Cursed be their anger for it was fierce: and their wrath, for it was cruel: I will divide them in Jacob and scatter them in Israel." Gen 49: 7.

I want to call your attention to the value of keeping covenant with God, and the natural curse that men bring upon themselves when they break covenant with God. Jacob's prophecy became a fact. Levi and Simeon had violated a covenant with God, and the old prophet's soul, as he looked down through the ages, saw what the end would be, and in his dying hour told them what the punishment of their sin would be.

The Covenant of Healing

Healing is one of God's covenants. God made a definite and specific Covenant of Healing, known in the Scripture as the covenant of "Jehovah-Rapha" or "The Lord thy Healer." You will find that Covenant in Exodus 15:26. There are four divisions to the Covenant of Healing.

First: "If thou wilt diligently hearken unto the voice of the Lord thy God."

Second: "And wilt do that which is right in his sight."

Third: "And wilt give ear to his commandments, and keep his statutes."

Fourth: "I will put none of these diseases upon thee,

which I have brought upon the Egyptians:] for I am the Lord that healeth thee."

Beloved, I want you to see that when men take upon themselves faith in the eternal God, as revealed through the Lord Jesus Christ for healing, they enter into a covenant relationship with God. It is a divine union. God has put Himself on record, and given eternal pledge as to His faithfulness concerning that Covenant. We then as intelligent men and women are invited to come into relationship with Him, and become partakers with Him in that Covenant.

Covenant More Than Just Healing, When Sick

This Covenant does not simply mean that when we are sick and dying, the Lord will come and heal us. That is a small portion of the Covenant of Healing. The Covenant has three great principles involved. The first is *DIVINE HEALING*. The second is a bigger thing than Divine Healing; it is *DIVINE HEALTH*. If God keeps your family or your city or your nation in Divine Health there is no need for Divine Healing. The third is DIVINE LIFE. Divine Life is greater than Divine Health. Divine Life is that union of the soul with God by which the recipient becomes the partaker of His life.

The Unholy Brotherhood

Now are involved the three underlying principles that unfold the whole subject of healing. They are Sin, Sickness and Death, an unholy brotherhood, the representatives of the Kingdom of Darkness. They are the children of the Devil and Disobedience. If you want to look for their parentage, Satan is their father and Disobedience is their mother, and out of this union, Sin, Sickness and Death are born. All three are specifically declared by the

Word of God to be the enemies of God. God hates sin, and God equally hates sickness, for sickness is incipient death.

The final result of the Redemption of Jesus is the destruction of these three enemies of God, this triumvirate of darkness! All the Christian world is clear on this point, that Jesus Christ came to redeem the world from sin. They may dispute His methods but on general principles they believe that Jesus Christ is the Redeemer from sin.

The Christian world is not so well agreed that He is the Redeemer from sickness. The Church was agreed on that question at one time. In the early centuries of the Church's history there was no other method of healing known among Christians, except healing through faith in the Lord Jesus Christ. John Wesley says, in his notes on the New Testament, under James 5:14-16: "The only system of physics known in the early church for four hundred years was the prayer of faith for the sick." The early Christians had a Remedy, bless God, but it was an eternal one, the living eternal Spirit of Christ in the world, and in their heart, and in their person, when they needed Him for healing. God's Remedy is a Person, not a material remedy. It is not an "it" but a "Him." Beloved, receive this Spirit of God into your heart, into your life, into your being.

The Omnipresence of God

Some one has given a definition for omni-presence, as we use that word to express an attribute of God, "Equally present everywhere." Omnipresent means equally present everywhere. Consequently there is no place to go from His Presence. David emphasized this truth in splendid form: "Whither shall I go from thy Spirit? or whither shall I flee from thy presence? If I ascend up into heaven thou art there: if I make my bed

in hell, behold, thou art there. If I take the wings of the
morning, and dwell in the uttermost part of the sea; even
there shall thy hand lead me, and thy right hand shall
hold me." Ps. 139:7-10. There was no place of which
the mind of the prophet could conceive, where God was
not present.

Sometimes people get an idea that the only place that
God is present is at church or in their home. A man was
seeking for salvation and he went out to his horse stable
to pray. God came to him, and the consciousness of salvation was born in his soul. Then ever afterward when
he was interested in anybody's salvation, he wanted to
take them to the horse stable. We ought to get it in our
mind that God can meet us any where. Blessed be God!

There is a great difference between accepting and
expecting. You must take Christ as your Healer—not as
an experiment. Have you really committed yourself to
the Lord as your Healer? Has there been a definite act
of commital to the Lord? If there has, it has settled in
your mind all questions of relying on other means for
healing.

Personal Testimony

I was sitting one morning, suffering terribly from a
disease with which I had been afflicted for nine years.
That morning as I sat in my chair I reviewed all the
failures of other remedies that had been used in my
family and my father's family. I could not recall a
single instance where we had received the least benefit.
We had buried four brothers and four sisters. Four other
members of the family were dying, chronic invalids. It
was a matter of life and death. Faith was beginning to
dawn. I suddenly made a decision that from then on I
was going to put my trust entirely in the Lord.

I did not then fully realize what I had done, but by
that decision of my soul, I had cut myself off forever from

the help of man. I had separated myself unto God. I had no one else to look to, for I had refused the help of man. I was not aware of having prayed at all. *I went about my affairs, and to my surprise I awoke to the fact that I was perfectly well.* I had not the least idea when it took place. It may have taken place so gradually that I was not aware of it. That is the value of committal.

A. B. Simpson says concerning the committal of the health of our bodies to the Lord: "It ought to be very deliberate and final, and in the nature of things it cannot be repeated." Separated unto Jesus Christ as your only Physician, for time and eternity. If a man commits himself once and for all to the woman he is going to marry, it is done; he cannot repeat it. If you commit yourself once and for all, and forever to Jesus as your Healer, it is done forever. As A. B. Simpson says, "Like the marriage ceremony it is the signalizing and sealing of a great transaction, and depends for its value upon the reality of the union which it seals."

Incident of the Boer War

In the Boer War of South Africa, the Boers held a mountain peak that commanded the country all around, and particularly the city of Ladysmith. It was known as Spoin Kop. Tugels River ran along side. One day in the midst of a tremendous charge, the British succeeded in breaking through and crossing the river on pontoon bridges, and taking possession of the mountain.

That night the Boers called a Council of War and it was decided that the repossession of Spoin Kop was necessary to the successful progress of the war. Realizing that the retaking of Spoin Kop would result in a tremendous slaughter, and the officers not wishing to take responsibility of ordering men to attack, they called for volunteers. The word was passed along, and those who wished to volunteer stepped out and took their place one

by one. They were committing themselves to life and
death. In the morning when the sun arose, the Boers were
in possession of Spoin Kop, but two out of three of both
Boer and British were dead. Men will do that for war's
sake.

It means something to commit yourself to the things
of this world. It ought to mean just as much, and a lot
more, to definitely commit yourself to the Lord Jesus
Christ. The definite act of receiving and accepting and
placing yourself in committal to the Lord, should be very
solemn and deliberate. And by the Grace of God I am
trying to bring to your hearts this splendid truth. If
you have been toying with the subject of healing, and
experimenting with God, end it, and commit yourself
in faith and love to Jesus Christ as your Healer, forever.
Then you have placed yourself on the ground of blessing.
You have placed yourself where the Lord meets you, or
rather you meet the Lord.

Chapter IV

NOT TRY BUT TRUST

Scripture reading: Numbers 12.

Our Scripture reading begins with the incident of Miriam and Aaron speaking against Moses. A great many people lose the blessing by getting themselves in other peoples affairs. The Lord has been trying from the very beginning to get folks to learn this truth. This is one of the most severe lessons in the Word of God on the disadvantage of sticking your nose into other people's affairs.

Aaron was the brother and Miriam was the sister of Moses. When Moses was called at the Burning Bush, he began to make excuses because of his slowness of speech, and God gave him his brother Aaron, saying, "He shall be thy spokesman unto the people." Moses was very meek above all the men that were upon the face of the earth. Vs. 3. No man in all history had so many reasons to get puffed up if he had been puffable. The little fellow puffs up—the big fellow puffs down. No man ever listened to such words as the Lord spoke to Moses. No one was ever dignified by the same commission that God gave to Moses. When God called him and sent him into Egypt, He spoke these most startling words to him, "Thou shalt be as God." His word became as God and his actions became the actions of God.

As the result of Miriam's words against Moses, she became a leper. "The cloud departed from off the tabernacle; and behold Miriam became leprous, white as snow: and Aaron looked upon Miriam, and, behold, she was leprous. And Aaron said unto Moses, Alas, my Lord, I beseech thee, lay not the sin upon us, wherein we have done foolishly, and wherein we have sinned . . ."

And so Moses prayed. His prayer is characteristic of

many prayers of the Bible. It is brief. It contains only eight words: "Heal her now, O God I beseech thee." With Aaron's whole-hearted confession, the heart of Moses was moved even as was the heart of God.

When You Pray Believe

I want to talk to you a little about this subject of prayer. It seems to me that this prayer of Moses is a wonderful example of that remarkable teaching of Jesus on the subject of faith, in the eleventh chapter of Mark. After cursing the fig tree, Jesus utilized the instance to give voice to the marvelous teaching on faith in God.

He said, "Verily, verily." When an oriental used these words, he raised his hands and gave it with the solemnity of an oath. Then He said that we are to do something. "When ye pray, BELIEVE THAT YE RECEIVE THEM, and ye shall have them." Mark 11:23-24. The Revised Version gives greater force to it. "When ye pray, believe that ye have received." When? Why bless your soul "when you pray." You have it; that is what it means. We used to have a little Englishman in our evangelistic party who would say to the people when they were praying, "Now let us stop praying for five minutes and BELIEVE GOD, and see what will happen." It is perfectly amazing the things that will happen when people will believe God.

The Soul Cry of a Brother

There is an attitude of faith, an opening of the soul to God, a Divine laying hold in the Spirit. I can imagine the soul cry of Moses under these circumstances. Miriam, his own sister, was now smitten and leprous, "white as snow." What were the feelings of his heart? I sometimes have thought that there was no other circumstance in my own life that ever called out so much faith in God and determination of soul to see God's Will done, as in the healing of a sister. One of my sisters and I had been chums from our childhood. She was a little older than I. The vision of Christ as the Healer had just been opened to my soul.

She was dying of an issue of blood. My mother called me one night and said, "John, if you want to see your sister alive you must come at once." When I arrived, my mother said, "You are too late, she is gone." I stepped to her bedside, and laid my hand on her forehead; it was cold and white. I slipped my hand down over her heart, and the heart had ceased to beat. I picked up a small mirror and held it over her mouth, but there was no discoloration. The breath was gone. I stood there stunned. Her husband knelt at the foot of the bed weeping. Her baby was asleep in the crib at the opposite side of the room. My old father and mother knelt sobbing at the side of the bed. They had seen eight of their children die; she was apparently the ninth. My soul was in a storm.

Just a few weeks before, my wife had been healed when almost dead. Prior to that, my brother had been healed, after having been an invalid for twenty two years. A short time before that, my older sister, with five cancers in the breast, who had been operated on five times and given up to die, was healed. As I looked at this sister I said, "O God, this is not your Will, I cannot accept it! It is the work of the devil and darkness." It is the devil who has the power of death."

I discovered this strange fact, that there are times when one's spirit lays hold on the spirit of another. Somehow I just felt my spirit lay hold of the spirit of that sister. And I prayed, "Dear Lord, she just cannot go." I walked up and down the room for some time. My spirit was crying out for some body with faith in God that I could call upon to help me. That was twenty-five years ago when the individual who trusted God for healing was almost an insane man in the eyes of the church and the world. Bless God it is different now. That is the advantage of having people who trust God, and walk out on God's lines, come together, stay together, and form a nucleus in society which has some force for God. I have no confidence or faith in those little efforts that people run after here and there. Most of them go up in vapor. If you want something done for God and humanity, put your hearts and hands together and your souls together. Organize your effort.

That baby's mother (referring to a baby in the audience) would not have been healed, except that a little nucleus determined to pray until the woman was healed, and they stayed in prayer all day Monday. At five o'clock they had the victory. It took them all day. I wish that we had spirituality and faith enough to look through the mists and see what was taking place all day long, until the powers of darkness were dispelled and the healing came.

As I walked up and down my sister's room, I could think of but one man who had faith on this line, That was John Alexander Dowie, six hundred miles away. I went to the phone, called Western Union and told them I wanted to get a telegram through to Doctor Dowie with an answer back as quickly as possible. I sent this wire:

"My sister has apparently died but my spirit will not let her go. I believe if you will pray, God will heal her."

I received this answer back:

"Hold on to God. I am praying. She will live."

I have said a thousand times, what would it have meant if instead of that telegram of faith, I had received one from a weakling preacher who might have said: "I am afraid you are on the wrong track," or "Brother, you are excited," or "The days of miracles are past."

It was the strength of his faith that came over the wire that caused the lightnings of my soul to begin to flash, and while I stood at the telephone and listened, the very lightnings of God began to flash in my spirit. I prayed, "This thing is of hell, it cannot be, it will not be. In the Name of Jesus Christ I abolish this death and sickness, and she shall live." And as I finished praying, I turned my eyes toward the bed, and I saw her eyelids blink. But I was so wrought up I said, "Maybe I am deceiving myself." So I stood a little while at the telephone, the lightnings of God still flashing through my soul. Presently I observed her husband get up and tiptoe to her head, and I knew that he had seen it. I said, "What is it Peter?" He replied, "I thought I saw her eyelids move." And just then they moved again. Five days later she came to father's home and the Lake family sat down to Christmas dinner, the first time in their life when they were all well.

Persistent Prayer Sometimes Necessary

Beloved, it is not our long prayers but our believing God that gets the answer. However, I want to help somebody who finds persistent prayer a necessity, as we all do sometimes. We have not the least idea of the powers of darkness against which we are praying. Paul says:

"We wrestle not against flesh and blood, but against principalities, against powers, against the rulers of darkness of this world, against spiritual wickedness in high places." Ephes. 6:12.

And sometimes you have to lay hold of God, and stay before God and stay through the blackness and through the darkness, and through the night of it, until the faith of God penetrates, and the work is done.

Daniel's Experience

Do you remember the experience of Daniel, one of the finest in the Book? He had to hear from heaven. He fasted and prayed twenty one days. On the twenty first day an angel came to him right out of heaven, and the angel said, "Daniel, a man greatly beloved . . . from the first day . . . thy words were heard." Not the last time you prayed but the very first. The answer was on the way from the day that the prophet began to chasten himself before God. But the Prince of Persia withstood the angel twenty one days. Finally Michael, the Archangel, was sent to assist and the answer came through to Daniel. (Dan. 10:11-14)

Michael is spoken of again and again as the Warrior Angel. He made war against the devil and cast him out of heaven. Get the circumstance. Daniel had prayed and God heard his prayer and answered it by sending an angel messenger. But the angel himself was held up on the way by some power of darkness, until reinforcements, even Michael one of the chief angels, came to his help. I wonder what was necessary to be accomplished in the minds of those interested, before God could answer that prayer?

You are praying for somebody, you are praying for your friend, for your brother, or for your son, or for your daughter who needs your love and faith. Beloved have faith in God to stay and pray until the Spirit has a chance to work out the problem. That is the issue. Keep right down to it. Do not let go. It is the Will of God; you have a right to the answer.

There is a ministry of intercession that comes from heaven. It is prayer by the Spirit of God. It is entering into the prayer spirit of the Holy Ghost. He prays. He prays for you. He prays for me, "with groanings that cannot be uttered." Our spirit in union with His, we enter into the ether of God, into the oneness of faith, the love of His Spirit. A lot of folks stop when they are half through. You hold on to God and pray through.

There are times like the one when my sister was restored, when the faith and the power of God come like the lightning flash; as to Moses when he prayed, "Heal her now, O God I beseech thee," and the healing was instant. There are times when it is only our humanity that prays. You know these times yourself when your soul does not enter into your prayer, much less your spirit. There are times when your soul prays. Then there is a prayer of your spirit—that deep quality of your life, deeper than the soul. O bless God there is still a prayer where the spirit of man and the Spirit of God unite and become one.

Now one can imagine as Moses prayed that day, how his soul must have been stirred. Here is his own sister, that woman who had stood by the river side when he was a babe, had put him in a basket, had hid him in the bulrushes and watched over his welfare. Don't think she wasn't interested in him. She had a sisterly and motherly affection for Moses. She wanted to keep him straight. She was afraid that he had made a great mistake in his marriage. Say beloved, are you a father or a mother and have laid such a tight hold on a loved one that you are afraid to leave them in the Hands of God? That is one of the hardest things that folks have to learn, just to take their hands off the other, and let God have them.

Experience of Stephen Merritt

Stephen Merritt was a godly undertaker in the city of New York. His dear old wife and he lived godly lives. They raised one son, and if there ever was a boy that strayed away from God it was Charley. Charley would get into some disreputable affair, and the police would come and say, "Charley has done so and so. It will take just so much money to get him out of this difficulty." The next week another would come along with something else, and so it went on and on. And the two old gray heads were praying and pouring out their tears for that boy's salvation.

One day as Stephen Merritt was sitting in his office and praying about his son, and the floor was wet with his tears, he heard the Voice of God saying, "How long have you been trying to save Charley?" He replied, "Lord, a long time." The Lord said, "Now if you are through, I will undertake." The old man considered, and it worked out in his soul in this way.

The police came and said, "Charley did so and so." He asked, "Who is Charley?" "Why he is your son."

"No, I have no son, Charley." That day as he had knelt there he said, "Lord, he is not my son any more. I give him over to you until he is saved." So he told the police, "No, I have no son." They looked at him and shook their heads. Then they sent another officer. But it was no use to go to him any more. It looked as if the old man had gone crazy.

About nine months passed, and one day an officer came with the report, "Charley has jumped off the Brooklyn bridge and is finished." He wanted the old man to have the river dragged to obtain the body. But the father said, "I have no son Charley. Drag the river if you want to." So they dragged the river but the body found was not Charley's. Three months more passed, and one day one of the clerks said, "There is one of your friends in the office." And when the old man went in, it was Charley. He was well dressed, clean faced, everything indicating the light of God. The son fell at his feet, kissed them and asked his forgiveness. He said in explanation, "Three months ago I was saved in a mission, but I did not want to come and see you until I came as a man."

The Human Clutch

Not only is it so in your prayers for others, but in your prayers for yourself; some of you are holding on to your sickness, or difficulty with such a clutch, and are so everlastingly conscious of it, that God cannot get it out of your hands. You are in the very same place spiritually that Stephen Merritt was. He was so determined to save his boy that he was just doing it himself, and God was not getting a chance.

Maybe you are holding on to sin with that same clutch. Maybe you are holding on to disobedience with that same clutch. Maybe it is your sickness. If there is something that is keeping you from getting blessed, let go and let your hands and heart open.

When I was a boy I used to visit the Soo locks at Sault Ste. Marie, Michigan, where my home was. One day a sailor was up in the masts; he lost his balance and shot over the ship into the water. Another sailor stood on the railing of the ship and watched him. He went down and came up, and went down and came up again, and everything was in foam around him. Still the fellow stood there. Then the chap went down the third time, limp, and just as he was disappearing, the second sailor shot down into the water, and came up with him. A couple of gentlemen standing by remarked, "That fellow has taken men out of the water before." He just waited until all the kick was taken out of him. Otherwise both might have been drowned.

A lot of us have to thrash and struggle and fight until the kick is all out of us before we are ready to let God take us. As a young fellow I was as proud as Lucifer —every Lake I ever knew was. Robert Burns wrote with his diamond on the window of an highland inn, "There is nothing here but highland pride, highland pride and poverty." It did not make any difference how poor they were. The hardest thing that I had to do was to make my surrender to God. Never touched whiskey in my life, never used tobacco, but that proud heart of mine had to struggle like a drowning man until I was ready to say, "Lord you save me." The final consummation came when

I knelt behind an old elm tree and poured out my heart to God, and made my surrender to Him. The light of heaven broke into my soul, and I arose from my knees, a son of God and I knew it.

Let God have you. Quit sweating, quit wrestling. About the most difficult class in the world to get healed is the Christian Scientist. Why? Because they work at it so hard. They have been reading so many lessons, and concentrating their minds on healing until almost exhausted. You have to lead them away from it all to that place where, "It is not TRY but TRUST." That is the secret of Christ's salvation; that is the secret of Christ's healing. It is not trying to get healed. It is trusting Him for it, and believing Him when He says He will do it, and the mind relaxes and the soul comes to rest.

Say, dear hearts, let go! Open your clutch! Let God take you. Let God have you, whether it is for your spirit, whether it is for your soul, whether it is for your body. No matter what, just let go. It is not TRY but TRUST. God be praised!

Chapter V

SPECIFIC AND DEFINITE GROUNDS FOR HEALING

The subject of Healing is treated in the Word of God on a scale of graduation from Genesis to Revelation. There is a graduation and development in the promises concerning healing; also in the distinct principles laid down by the Lord by which healing is received.

The real climax of the ministry of healing as shown in the Word of God, comes from the Baptism of the Holy Ghost, as received on the day of Pentecost, when believers became infilled, inhabited, indwelt by the Living Spirit of the Living God.

The Purpose of Jesus Christ

The purpose for which Jesus Christ lived and died on the Cross, descended into the grave, ministered to the dead who died in the hope of His Coming transferring them to His own glory, arose from the dead, and His final ascent to the throne of God, was for one purpose. That one purpose was that He, Jesus Christ the Son of God, might be endowed with the Gift of the Holy Ghost and have the right as the Saviour of men, to minister it to His followers for evermore.

Without that final climax at the Throne of God, all the rest would have been valueless. The Promise of the Father was fulfilled to Jesus Christ Himself. And Christ as Saviour and Redeemer of Mankind, exercising the Power of God, proceeded to minister it to His followers from on High.

Healing Known in the Patriarch Age

Away back in the days of the patriarchs, leading up to the days of Moses, the subject of healing was apparently just as well known as among us. Men have trusted God from time immemorial. It started with the need of mankind. The first record of actual healing is at the time the wives of Abimelech were healed in answer to the prayers of Abraham. The next example is the healing of Sarah from barrenness, when she was ninety years old. It was not just an ordinary healing, but a creative work. The processes of nature that had died and passed in her life, were restored by the action of God Almighty, and she was able to bear children at ninety years. Rachel is another example of healing of barrenness, recorded in the Book of Genesis.

Separation By Covenant

When you come to the Book of Exodus, a great phase of healing is opened. Israel has left Egypt. They have crossed the Red Sea and are now in the wilderness. They are away from earth's methods, and from oppressive laws. A lot of Christians have not gotten that far yet. Their Christianity is not of the vital, practical order. They have vital faith for the salvation of their soul when they are dying. Lots of people have a salvation that will do a lot of things when they are dead. But Christ's salvation will do a marvelous lot for you while you are alive! The dead end of it will take care of itself. Whatever revelation God has for you and me when we die will be revealed in due order. Our life is here now to perform in us what He has promised.

So in the 15th of Exodus we have the remarkable record of a whole nation, two million five hundred thousand of them—old gray-haired men and women, middle-aged men of war, young men, wives, children and unborn babes, accepting this Covenant with God, having no other healer than the Lord.

No man or woman over twenty years of age at the time they left Egypt ever entered Canaan, except Joshua and Caleb. The nation that entered in was a new-born nation, born under the Covenant of the eternal God, never having known any other system of healing, except faith in God. That Covenant was given after the peculiar testing of the people at the Waters of Marah.

Healing of the Bitter Waters
(Exod. 15:23-25)

God had brought them through the Red Sea by a Divine miracle. They stepped out a new-born nation. The Pillar of Cloud stopped at the waters of Marah. Marah means "bitter." When they came to examine the springs, the water was bitter. You can imagine the consternation that followed. Think of the mothers wanting drink for their children. Yea, old men who were panting for thirst. And here this strange experience, the Pillar of Cloud stops at these undrinkable springs, Marah!

I suppose all the human remedies of mankind were suggested. One thing sure, they commenced to growl. The growlers are always on hand. Moses was a hero; we have a few hundred to growl at us, but here he had two million five hundred thousand to growl all at one time; I presume committees were waiting on him. One said, "Moses, what in the world did you stop here for?" "O the Pillar of Cloud stopped here." "Well something has gone wrong with the machinery; it is out of order. God would not have stopped here." Perhaps they said, "Do you think that we had better manufacture a drilling machine?" Or, "Don't you think that we better send out scouting parties to find a spring somewhere around the neighborhood?" Men have always been human.

Moses had a way of getting difficulties settled that I wish we knew more about. While the rest were grouching, he went off to pray, and to get in touch with God. A lot of folks pray but do not get in touch with God. They operate the machinery of prayer at one end, but never get any response from the other end. Real prayer is communion with God, not just praying words, but getting an answer from heaven. "The prayer of faith shall save the sick." God never promised healing through any other prayer than the prayer of faith. Lots of people pray prayers. Our books are full of prayers. We are splendid beggars, magnificent beggars, but poor believers. About the hardest thing to get hold of is a good old-fashioned Christian who believes God.

I sat by the bedside of an old Methodist lady the other day, a good woman, and I haven't a doubt of her salvation. But when I knelt to pray for her, all she would say was, "O Jesus heal me, O Jesus heal me." And she kept it up until it seemed to me the Lord Himself must be wearied. After awhile I tried to get her out of it. I said, "Dear sister, you do not have to beg the Lord to heal you. He died to do that. He is waiting to do it." She took a long breath and said, "What will I do?" I said, "Quit begging and believe God for a little while, and see if something will not happen."

Beloved, whether you get an answer from heaven or not is dependent on the set of your soul. When your heart is set and fixed in God in believing faith, something will take place. In Chemistry there has to be a union of substances before there is any action. Paul said, "The Word spoken them did not profit." Why? "Not being mixed with faith." The Spirit of God has a Divine quality. The spirit of faith in the heart of man is the human quality necessary to ignite the Spirit of God, and give it Divine action in your soul. "Without faith it is impossible to please God." God demands faith. According to the degree of faith in your soul, so that action, or interaction, of the Spirit of God in your life for healing will be great or small. Little faith, little healing; much faith, much healing; no faith, no healing. That is the principle.

Where Jesus Placed Responsibility

Some teachers endeavor to throw the weight of responsibility on the patient. The Word of God does not do so. The Word of God is the finest straight up-and-down exposition of real manliness that I know of anywhere. Christ put the burden of responsibility upon the disciples themselves. When He met faith He commended it in those special cases. But He said to the disciples, "Behold I give you power and authority," and, "I send you to heal the sick and cast out devils." And they went and healed the people.

To the Seventy He said, "Go into the cities round about. Heal the sick that are therein: then say to them, the Kingdom of God is come nigh to you." That was to be their explanation. I trust that some day we will have a missionary army equipped by the power of God, that will go and heal the heathen, and discover that their message will have strength and power in the lives of the nations that it now lacks. A God without power to heal a sick heathen's body is a poor recommendation of His ability to save his soul.

When you go down among the Portland heathen you can do just the same. Paul Rader was preaching in the slums, and some of the big preachers went down to hear him. They thought the result marvelous, and they invited him to come and preach in one of their big churches. He broke loose and gave them the same kind of preaching he had given in the slums. The Board took him in hand and said, "Rader, over there in the slums it was wonderful, and this message moved the people; but this is a different class of people, and we do not think this is the kind of message for this congregation." One member of the board was a doctor. Rader said, "Doctor when you have a case of diphtheria in the slums and another on Locust Street, do you give a different remedy to the patient in the slums than the one on Locust Street?"

"No," he said, "I give the same thing." "All right, I guess if the disease is the same, the same remedy will work," said Rader.

God's One and Only Remedy

God has only one remedy. He never had any other. God's remedy is the Lord Jesus Christ. The Lord Jesus Christ ministered to your soul by the Spirit is the only redemptive power that can redeem the soul from sin. God never had any other remedy for sickness either. That remedy is the Lord Jesus Christ, ministered to the natures of men by the Spirit.

Here is this whole nation of two million five hundred thousand, assembled at the Waters of Marah. God performed a miracle and the waters are healed and sweetened. First, as an example of His Power. Second, in order to encourage the faith of the people to trust Him anywhere, under any circumstances.

Trust Both Spirit and Body to God

Did you ever try to deal with a lot of Spiritualists and get them saved? They fool around with spirits until they are candidates for the asylum, obsessed and possessed; then they want deliverance. And they are the most difficult people to keep steady in God and going along in the line of faith. They have been educated to throw their nature open to every dirty thing in the form of spirit, and to admit it. It is natural for them to do it. While the real Christian is taught to keep his nature free from any power that contaminates. Do not let everything that comes to your ears take possession. Put the bars of your soul up and shut out that which is unholy and unclean and untrue. Open your spirit to the Holy Spirit, the truth and love of God, and let God in and keep the rest out.

A lot of Christians have a little medicine god behind the door, and every time they have a stomach ache they are open to temptation and are about in the same position as the Spiritualists. They have been so used to letting in their dope god, they can hardly get along without him. You have to line these people up every little while, and bless them, and thresh the life nearly out of them, until they can stand on their feet and keep away from their medicine god, and trust, not try the Living God.

You ask what right I have to say that? In the fifteenth Chapter of Exodus we have the Covenant of Healing that God gave to the nation of Israel, after they had crossed the Red Sea and were at the Waters of Marah.

The Lord Almighty signed that Covenant as Jehovah-Rapha, the Lord Thy Healer, and the people of God lived for many consecutive years under that Covenant. Israel never had any other physician for centuries. The high, the low, the rich and the poor, the kings and the beggars put their trust in the living, eternal God. Down the line there was only one record of a man violating that covenant with God, and that was the case of Asa, king of Judah. His offense was so noticeable that it finds a place in the record of the Chronicles. When diseased in his feet he failed to trust God, but sought the physicians, and he "slept with his fathers." 2 Chron. 16:13.

It is a poor business to mix with unbelievers, unless you keep the spirit of your faith. Solomon got to marrying. He went down in Egypt and married a batch of Egyptian wives, who brought their heathen physicians with them to his court at Jerusalem, and introduced into Israel the practice of medicine. Eventually Asa the king abandoned trust in God, for the heathen method. Drugs have always been the unbeliever's way of healing. God always was and is the real Christian's remedy.

David gave the most wonderful health report that was ever written. He says, "There was not one feeble person among their tribes." Ps. 105:37. Some health, glory to God! God gave this Covenant, and He said, "As long as you keep it you will be blessed, and when you violate it, the natural consequences will follow." The natural consequences are curse, degradation of life, sickness, disease and all the wretchedness that is associated with it.

A Great Demonstration

I attended one of the great Dowie demonstrations of healing some years ago at the Chicago Auditorium, when at a certain moment, ten thousand people, standing, testified to their healing. There were five bushel baskets filled with cards containing the names of sixty thousand people healed by God. At the same time, while the audience of ten thousand stood testifying to the power of God, Dowie turned over these baskets containing sixty thousand names, making a total of seventy thousand testimonies to healing.

I do not know what other people's opinion of the Dowieites is, but you can go to their city (Zion, Ill.) today, 1923, and look at the vital statistics, and you will find that their death rate is lower than in any other city of the land with the same population. It testifies that the individual who puts his trust in God and God alone, is a sane individual and is exercising good common sense.

Why do you come to God in repentance and honesty of heart? That you may become free from sin. Why do you through prayer and spiritual labor and tears endeavor to keep your life purged from all contamination of sin, but for the reason that by the Grace of God you may command a greater degree of His heavenly presence and power?

Christians have seen the subject of healing as the Grace of God, but have not realized that it is a science as well as a grace. I tell people that there is not only a grace of healing but an ART of healing. It is grace because it belongs to God and the quality of healing virtue is the Spirit of the Living God Himself. But if you are going to discuss it from the side of art, then the individual who understands how to open his nature to God, so as to let that lifestream pass through from himself to others, is practicing the art of healing. Repentance and all associated with it, is in order that our hearts may be opened to Him in the greatest possible fulness.

Restitution Brings Healing

On one occasion a gentleman suffering from diabetes came to me. He explained his condition and showed me a chart by the State Board of Health showing his condition for months past. He said, "I do not want to die. I have come for help." I said, "Dear Brother, the Lord has help for you." So we knelt down by my office chair and began to pray. As we prayed, all I could see was $5000.00. I asked, "Brother, what is this $5000, that is always coming up before my soul? Have you stolen $5000?" He broke down and said, "Yes, that is my difficulty. I stole $5000.00 from my widowed sister-in-law when my brother died." I said, "Have you that amount in the bank?" He replied, "Yes." I asked, "How long ago did this take place?" He answered, "Eight years and three months." I told him, "If you want healing, you sit down here and write a check for that amount, including the interest." He wrote the check and I saw that it was mailed. I said, "Now brother, come back." He was going away in tears. "You will find you have some faith in God now." He knelt by the desk chair again and it was not like it was in the beginning. His heart was right and repentance and restitution had been made; his heart had been opened up and he prayed like a good old Methodist. That man is one of my fast friends and he is well.

Bless God, if you want some of the lovely things from Him, you go home and straighten up with the grocery man and every one else. And if you want to be honest and haven't the money, call them up and talk to them like a man. Keep yourself square with God and with man, and He will bless you.

Healing is not always obtained by saying prayers. It is obtained by obeying God. God wants the Christian to set up a standard of righteousness according to the standard of the Word of God, and then to live it, bless God. The church, not recognizing this truth has almost disregarded the teachings and lessons of the Old Testament and does not understand to this day what the difficulty is.

One day the British government got to wondering what was the cause of their troubles. Some of the members of parliament got to reading the Old Testament and the national laws of health. They said, "We have inherited the curses but missed the blessings." They wanted to know what they could do to inherit the blessings and get rid of the curses. They had labor trouble, land legislation, the courts were full of disputes about personal rights. They had disease. They went as far as to appoint a committee to look into the matter and bring back a report. Then came the World War and the matter was shelved. Beloved if we wish Divine health in our bodies and lives, we need to get back to old-fashioned obedience to the Word of God.

Immunity from Disease

When we began to trust the Lord for healing, and God alone, twenty five or more years ago, my wife and I had faith that when we were sick the Lord would heal us. The result was that when the measles broke out, our children would come home with the measles. The Lord would heal them. That went on for several years, and one evening when I came home, I discovered that two of the children had smallpox. That was the limit. If there is anything my soul hates it is the smallpox. Discovering the children had smallpox, we claimed God's promise in Psalms 91 which says, "Neither shall any plague come nigh thy dwelling," and thus banished sickness from our home.

Very few Christians are aware that the blessed Word of God gives such an amazing example of healthfulness as is told in the history of Israel. There is only one example that superseded it, and that is in the Christian Church during the first three centuries. The millions of Christians who lived during that time all trusted the Lord for healing.

Scientific Application of God's Spirit

If we could make the world understand the pregnant vitality of the Spirit of God, men would discover that healing is not only a matter of faith, and a matter of the Grace of God, but a perfectly scientific application of God's Spirit to man's needs. The Spirit of God is just as tangible as electricity is. You handle it, you minister it to another, you receive it from God through faith and prayer, your person becomes supercharged with it. The old apostle took handkerchiefs or aprons, held them in his hands until the handkerchiefs or aprons were supercharged with the Spirit of God. Then they were sent to the sick, the sick were healed and the demons were cast out of them. Acts 19:12.

Chapter VI

HEZEKIAH'S SICKNESS AND HEALING

Our lesson today is the story of Hezekiah's sickness and healing. The story is told in three different places in the Scriptures. In Second Kings 20, we read one of the accounts:

"In those days was Hezekiah sick unto death. And the prophet Isaiah the son of Amoz came to him, and said unto him, Thus saith the Lord, Set thine house in order; for thou shalt die and not live.

Then he turned his face to the wall, and prayed unto the Lord, saying, I beseech thee, O Lord, remember how I have walked before thee in truth and in a perfect heart, and have done that which is good in thy sight. And Hezekiah wept sore. . . .

And afore Isaiah had gone out into the middle court, the word of the Lord came to him saying, Turn again and tell Hezekiah . . . Thus saith the Lord . . . I have heard thy prayer, I have seen thy tears: behold I will heal thee." Vss. 1-5.

How quickly his cry reached heaven! How speedily God sent the answer! God has His eye on us hasn't He? We are inclined to feel some times that by some spiritual telephonic communication the Lord hears our prayer, but we forget that He sees our tears also. What a wonderful lesson is contained in that last verse. After he was healed he was to go up to the house of the Lord and give thanks. God was instructing him. A whole lot of folks have taken their healing like a dog or an animal and have run off with it. They have never even taken pains to give thanks in "the house of the Lord." It betokens a low state of mind and an ungrateful state of soul. Lack of gratitude is most repellent. It bespeaks a brutish person. Beloved we need in these sodden days, when it seems as though the light of the Spirit has almost gone out, to be careful and by the Grace of God keep in harmony with the Spirit of faith in God, and show our gratitude to Him.

It was just like our Father to give more than we asked for. We read later that the Assyrians came with a vast army, and of the marvelous deliverance by the Lord through His power. God kept His Word.

Hezekiah's Prayer

I want to call your attention to Hezekiah's prayer as recorded in Isaiah 38. He is recounting the things that went on in his soul while that battle for his life raged.

"The writing of Hezekiah king of Judah, when he had been sick, and was recovered of his sickness: I said in the cutting off of my days, I shall go to the gates of the grave: I am deprived of the residue of my years. I said, I shall not see the Lord . . . in the land of the living: I shall behold man no more with the inhabitants of the world. Mine age is departed, and is removed from me as a shepherd's tent: I have cut off like a weaver my life: he will cut me off with pining sickness." Isa. 38:9-12.

There are tremendous lessons associated with these simple statements. You go back in his life and you will see that through disobedience to God, sickness had come upon him, and he was now confessing his sin. He is not blaming God for it, but himself. That is the spirit of confession. "I have cut off like a weaver my life . . . O Lord, I am oppressed; undertake for me."

Coming to the End of Ourselves

Sometimes we sing, "when we get to the end of the way." There is a "getting to the end of the way" with ourselves, or an end to ourselves and our self-effort, where in the fullness of our hearts we cry, "LORD UNDER-TAKE FOR ME." Sometimes in our strength and the

inspiration of faith that is in our soul, we put up a
great battle. Again and again I have faced death, and I
have won by sheer persistence of tenacious faith. But
there came an occasion when I had no strength to pray.
That was when I had the flu. I went down into very
death until my toenails turned black, and death proceeded
up my body until it reached my abdomen. My fingers
died, my arms, my shoulders died. Death struck the top
of my head and came down through me to my heart. My
brain was so weak I could scarcely think, let alone pray.

My wife was worn out, and had been persuaded to
sleep downstairs. Everybody was worn out caring for the
sick through the epidemic. My nurse, Mrs. Mero, sat
down in a rocking chair and went sound asleep. I wanted
to be alone with God, so I was glad she was asleep. After
awhile it got to the place where I could scarcely think.
I could not pray and I settled down in the pillows like
a child. I could not speak a prayer, but I just thought,
"Lord I am too weak to pray. I am just going to cuddle
down in your arms. It is all right with me Lord, but is
it really time to go home? I am ready, but Lord, I do not
believe it is. I have not begun to do the things that my
heart has been asking to do in life."

And as I lay there perfectly still, after about thirty
minutes, I heard the Voice of God speak to my soul. The
Voice was rebuking the disease. "Thus far shalt thou go
and no farther." And I rose to health from that minute.

Death Bed Resolutions

You know there are death bed resolutions as well as
death bed repentances. Hezekiah, in his prayer for healing
had promised the Lord, "I shall go softly all my years in
the bitterness of my soul." Vs. 15. I wonder how many
like Hezekiah, have sworn to "walk softly" before God
and then have forgotten? It reminds me of the lines:
"The devil was sick, the devil a saint would be. The

devil was well, the devil a saint was he." The sad record
is that Hezekiah did not keep his vow. We read in 2
Chron. 32:24-26: "But Hezekiah rendered not again
according to the benefit done unto him: for his heart
was lifted up: therefore there was wrath upon him, and
upon Judah, and Jerusalem. Notwithstanding Hezekiah
humbled himself for the pride of his heart, both he and
the inhabitants of Jerusalem so that the wrath of the
Lord came not upon them in the days of Hezekiah."

After wrath threatened, then he proceeded to humble
himself. Lots of folks do that. It is better to learn to walk
at the feet of the Lord, so that wrath does not come at
all. What a call there is in this lesson to that humbleness
of walk before the Eternal God, through whom we receive
blessing.

The Lesson of the Sign of the Sun Dial

There is another lesson, the importance of a healing in
God's sight, which seems to me the deepest and most
powerful in all this story. When Isaiah came to the bedside to tell him what the Lord had said, that he would not
die but live, and that the Lord would add fifteen years to
his life, Hezekiah said, "What shall be the sign that the
Lord will heal me, and that I shall go up into the house of
the Lord the third day?" The answer was given that the
shadow should return backward on the sun-dial ten
degrees. Vss. 8-11.

Think of the magnitude of the thing that Isaiah the
prophet was proposing—the fact that the shadow should
return backward ten degrees. There is only one other
incident of this order in all the Word of God. It was
when Joshua prayed, and the sun stood still, and the
moon was stayed during the progress of one of their
battles, until they had won that battle. See Joshua 10:12,
13.

This incident of the sign given to Hezekiah struck

me with new force today. Mrs. Lake read this story as
we rode along the highway between Eugene and Portland.
She said, "Is it not strange that there should be such a
tremendous sign given for a healing?" It would naturally
seem as if the healing were an insignificant matter compared to the sign that the prophet gave as an assurance of
the healing.

Beloved does it not prove that in the sight of God,
the king's healing, or the healing of anyone else, is as
great and wonderful in the mind of God as the moving
of the sun backward ten degrees, or the staying of the
sun and the moon in the Valley of Ajalon? It required
the same action of the mind of God to bless Hezekiah and
heal him as it did to turn the sun back and record it on
the sun dial.

Dear ones, I wonder if we are not in the habit of just
accepting the wonderful healings of God, and running
off with them as though we had a toy of some kind, and
as though the Eternal God of the universe had not taken
time and pains to heal us? Oh how we forget that these
are matters of life and death. So important is our healing
in the mind of God that He would stop the revolution of
a world if necessary to accomplish it.

Yesterday afternoon I went out with a group of
ministers to pray for some sick folks around the city. In
one home we ministered to a whole household. Some
members of the family had recently died, several others
were confirmed invalids. It made my soul sick. I said
to one of the ministers, "Such a sight as this reveals our
present-day Christianity as a helpless, wretched force.
What would happen if Jesus Christ came into this house?
He would show us what Christianity is by healing this
family. Is it not time that we came out of our wretched
theological debates, and get hold of the Eternal God, and
called the power of Christ down upon a house like this?"
That house was afflicted with a spirit of infirmity. The

whole family was in the same condition. It is only the
Eternal God and His eternal power that will blast the
curse of sickness from the homes of people, cast it out
and set mankind free.

Think of five or six splendid ministers sitting around
in a town debating all kinds of little quibblings, such as
"Will the Lord heal?" "Are the days of miracles past?"
"Will He heal this way, or will He heal that way, or
will He heal at all?" Beloved for the sake of a dying
suffering world, pay the price, get God's power, and set
the prisoners free!

Think of Jesus Christ coming to the world after these
hundreds of years and finding the church asleep and the
people dying in the toils of suffering! I wonder if we
appreciate the light of God that has come to us? I wonder
if we appreciate what it means to have homes where
there is health, and where there is holiness?

The Law of Death

Hezekiah's sickness was "unto death." And so God
in His love sent the prophet to him saying, "Set thine
house in order; for thou shalt die, and not live." You may
have brought upon yourself a tremendous curse just like
Hezekiah did. For his own sin, according to his own
confession, was the cause of his calamity. What is your
sin? Is it carelessness and inactivity of the soul, that
peculiar lethargic condition that steals over the heart
of the Christian, until something drastic comes along to
wake him up? So God said, "Thou shalt die and not live."
This is the law of sin. That is the law of circumstance.
According to every known law, he would die. God knew
it, God wanted him to be ready. It was not a decree of
God. He was not killing him or giving him a sickness.
That was the development that came from sin. God has
a care for those we leave behind. Hezekiah had a kingdom to be continued when he was gone.

Cause of Sickness

I want to tell you, when you begin to analyze the subject of sickness, you will discover that usually the difficulty is that there is sin behind it. Not necessarily that there is an act of sin or some personal sin, but more likely the laziness of our soul, or the inactivity of our spirit, or neglect of God's Word, or neglect of faith and love and prayer. These are the things that usually underlie and generate difficulties in men's lives.

The Healing Power of Tears

Next, God will heal you when you repent and confess your sin, and your need of Him. Now God loves to answer prayer. How God loves an honest repentance. How God loves that soul that is big enough to pour out his heart in prayer, and pour out his tears with it! We do not see enough of tears these days. I was talking to a brother about the Baptism of the Holy Ghost, and I said, "One of the things we need is a baptism of tears." A baptism of tears for the lethargic state of our life, and the curse our souls have tolerated. My how the church needs to confess!

Have you been weeping over your sins lately, or over your sicknesses? Bless God if you have, the Lord has heard your prayers, He has seen your tears.

When we get sick, the trouble is we do not get to the place of tears. Usually before Christians get halfway there, they are ready to run to the hospital and get something cut out. Let the operation take place in the head and the heart, and the disease will disappear. Bless God. Add a few tears to your prayers and see if it will not bring the desired result from heaven. I cannot remember a circumstance when I prayed for a soul that was broken in spirit and bathed in tears, that was not healed. It is beautiful to see the hardness of men's nature dissolve in tears, when they are the tears of true repentance unto God.

Incident of Woman's Healing

I was preaching in Chicago on one occasion when a dear woman came to the altar. She told me she had been seeking healing for seven years. She had been everywhere. She had been prayed for dozens of times. I watched her for awhile but I did not offer to pray for her. Brother Fockler and I strolled off after the meeting. He said, "Lake, you did not pray for that woman." I said, "I felt in my soul it would be a good thing to leave her alone for awhile." After an hour or so we came back, and that poor soul was still kneeling there. But the tears were flowing until there was a puddle upon the floor. The next meeting was about to begin, but as I took up my hymn book I saw that poor soul and I said, "Brother Fockler come on, we are going to pray for her now." We laid hands upon her head, and as we did, the fire of God struck her; that was the end of her trouble forever. She was instantly healed.

Beloved, mix your tears with your prayers when you come to God. If your prayers are deep enough in your spirit, so that they bring forth tears, bless God, it means God is finding a way down into your life. God has a difficult time getting the rubbish cleared out of our mind, out of our heart, and getting us down into the solid of our life.

How many of you have confessed your sin to God, who have come for healing? How many of you have really asked God to save you out of your sins and meant it? How many of you have really put yourself on God's altar? That is what gets the pathway clear. God's chariot will come down the road when the stones are taken away. Blessed be God.

Chapter VII

THE TANGIBILITY OF THE SPIRIT

It is one of the most difficult things in all the world for people who are not familiar with the ministry of healing to comprehend that the Spirit of God is tangible, actual, a living quantity, just as real as electricity. just as real as any other native force. Yea and a great deal more so. The life principle that stands behind all manifestations of life everywhere.

Your spirit is the life quality of you, the life principle that gives you action. Not just your mind, but the inbreathed Spirit of God, the breath that God breathed into man. That is eternal. Take this outward man and bury him in the ground, and the worms will eat him. But they will not eat the real man—the one that lives within. So few have any conception of giving that inner man his proper place, or recognize his divine right to rule and govern the whole being.

Now the secret of becoming a Christian is simply that you give God the right to come into your life and indwell your entire being. You have a spirit before God comes in to save you. It is a God-breathed spirit. The eternal, that God breathed into you in the beginning. It took that to make a man of you. That is not salvation. But when Jesus Christ comes into a soul to save a man, His Spirit is born into your nature in saving Grace. He takes possession of your spirit, your soul, and your body, and salvation is the most real thing under heaven. Bless God!

Incident of the Man Who Fell In the River

On one occasion I was crossing one of the bridges in Chicago, when a man fell into the river. That was when all the sewage of Chicago went into the river. A man with more presence of mind than I had, grabbed a rope from a dray and succeeded in getting him out, but he was unconscious. A doctor had been called and he put the fellow across a barrel and began to churn him. A gentleman said, "Well thank God, he is saved." But the doctor said, "Not so fast. We have gotten him out of the river; now we must get the river out of him." And he proceeded to get some of that black, inky river out of the man, and get the air into his lungs.

A lot of people in that sense are saved. They have taken hold of God by faith that when they die they will go to heaven, and live with the Lord. But there is a bigger thing than that. The salvation of the Lord Jesus Christ is in "getting the river out of you." Getting the frogpond out of your spirit, so it is pure and sweet like the Spirit of God. Out of your mind so that it is healed, and you have thoughts of God and consciousness of God. All the dirty rotten filths cleansed out of you by the power of God. That is salvation. Jesus never taught any other kind. He taught a salvation for the spirit, for the soul, and for the body, all one glorious manifestation of the redeemed man, Bless God! My heart just rings and my soul just chimes with heaven on that conception of real salvation. That is where the world fell down. That is where the church fell down, when the conception of real salvation deteriorated from that high standard and came down the scale until it was just a squeezing into heaven, and the pungent force of His Redeeming Grace was lost sight of. It has been coming back very gradually.

We who have been following the lessons of the past few weeks in the Old Testament have been getting the foundation truths upon which the whole structure of faith for healing is based—on the experiences of the Patriarchs, on the Covenant that God made with the Children of Israel. "If thou wilt diligently hearken to the voice of the Lord thy God." That is the first principle of healing—obedience to the Will of God.

My, when people get to living in harmony with God
and God's Word, they have eliminated nearly one half the
causes of disease already! A man came into my office on
Tuesday and said, "O, I am going crazy." I remarked,
"Well you look like it." He added, "I feel like going out
and drowning myself." I answered, "Sit up like a man
and tell me what is the matter with you." He told me,
"My wife is trying to leave me." I replied, "Well the
remarkable thing is that she is just trying to leave; it is
a wonder that she doesn't just go." "Now," I said, "I
will tell you what you need. You need to get down before
God and repent of your sin and get right with God. When
you do you will be right with your wife and everybody
else. Until then you will have hell in your home. It is
you that is making it and taking it there." Well, bless
God, he did, and he is a saved man and has a saved home,
and the family has not gone to wreck.

Yes friends, obedience to the Word of God is the first
principle upon which relationship with God is established.

Normal Way to Be Healed

A lady here had a brother who was dying of dropsy.
He came here and began to recover for a week or two,
until conviction for sin came, and this absorbed his mind
and soul. Then his body began to grow worse. He went
clear down to death. Then he threw up his hands and
yielded to God. His soul was satisfied. Then the virtue
of the Lord came and healed him.

We are glad God undertakes to save people by any
method, but the natural and normal way is to come and
confess your sin, and get right with God. You are then
on believer's ground, your heart is at rest, your soul is
at peace, and you have a consciousness of God's salvation
in your spirit. Then faith for healing is natural.

We were ministering to a dear man who was dying
of a chronic disease. He kept on dying. After awhile he

began to get anxious about his salvation. That anxiety developed until it was absorbing his soul. I said, "There is no use praying for his healing. He will never be healed until his heart comes into rest with God." I told the brother who went out to see him to pray the power of God upon him to save him from sin. When he came back he reported that the sick man's face was aglow. The Lord had come and saved him from his sins and then healed him. "For the law of the spirit of life in Christ Jesus hath made me free from the law of sin and death." In such a Scripture as the above you have one of those wonderfully condensed statements which in a few words reveal the greatest spiritual principles. Another one is, "In the beginning God created the heaven and the earth." Still another is found in 1 Cor. 8:6, "But to us there is but one God, the Father, of whom are all things, and we in him; and one Lord Jesus Christ, by whom are all things, and we by him." God the original, from Whose life and nature and character and substance Jesus Christ the Creator made all things. So he who prays takes of the Spirit and Substance of Christ and by his faith forms or creates his soul's desires, whether for holiness or for health.

Men, by the action of the will, take themselves out of the control of the power of the law of sin and death, and by the action of their will place themselves consciously in union and in touch with the law of the Spirit of Life.

The Law of Levitation

We read of an individual about the Sixteenth Century who was known as the Flying Monk. The peculiarity was that in certain spiritual states, the man would rise from his chair and float around the room. On one occasion when some royalty was visiting, it is said that he ascended into the air and went out the window. It has been reasoned that this man put himself in contact with some law of levitation, and it lifted him out of his chair and carried him out of the window.

Suppose he could have remained in touch with that law. I wonder where he would have gone? Back in the Old Testament the prophets went out to look for Elijah. They said, "Peradventure the Spirit of the Lord hath taken him up, and cast him upon some mountain." They were more intelligent about spiritual laws than this generation. But Elisha said, "He is not in the mountains, for when I was down by the river the glory of God came down from heaven, and he stepped into the chariot and he has gone on to glory."

Are You Tied to Something?

We walk through this life with our minds closed, our hearts centered in this old world. How men's hearts and lives are tied to this world. The manager of a theater sent for me, and I prayed for three people in his office. He said, "I have sixteen theaters and every morning I get a report from each institution by telegraph or long distance telephone giving me all the details of the conditions of business. I am just weighted down with it." I said, "Dear Lord, here is a man with his whole nature absorbed in this one thing, the management of a group of theaters. He has no vision of God or life or any thing. Here is a man living in that wretched little circle, and all he knows is to keep his theater machine going."

What are you tied to, Brother or Sister? A little home along the highway, or on one of those streets? You cannot take it to glory with you. One of these days you are going to die, and there you will leave it and where will you be? Most of us have more consideration for the old house and lot, or a few other trifles than we have for ourselves. Jesus tried to bring that lesson to us by saying,

"The life is more than meat, and the body is more than raiment."

The Christian stands out as the revelation of the divine power of Jesus Christ to come into the spirit of man, and change it and make it sweet and lovely like God Himself. To come into the mind of man, and take possession of all its faculties. To come into the nature of man and change it by the power of God until his thoughts are pure, holy, and lovely. To come into his old diseased body until God's action revolutionizes every cell of the blood. I believe that when the Blood of Jesus Christ is applied to a man's nature, spirit, soul and body, that when his sin is forgiven, the effects of that sin should be eliminated from his life. This may not be true in all Christian lives because we have not been educated in our Christian faith to believe with the same force and power for physical cleansing, as we have for the cleansing of our soul. But the Word of God says, "I will cleanse their blood that I have not cleansed: for the Lord dwelleth in Zion." Joel 3:21.

It is a small matter for God to perform that operation. The whole purpose of salvation is to stop the sin and disease process in man. Men live like animals. I do not mean coarsely or vulgarly. They eat, sleep, entertain themselves, labor, but they are not in touch with God at all. Finally man awakens. Like the old colored preacher who was telling of the prodigal son. He said, "He took off his coat and spent that. Then he took off his vest and spent that. Then he took off his shirt, and when he took off his shirt, he came to his self." We come to ourselves in various ways.

Benjamin Franklin believed he could bottle electricity. He had a conception that it was real and tangible and could be handled. He believed that the lightning was the same as electricity, so he made a kite and attached a key to the string. With his hand he drew a spark from the

key. The result of this experiment revolutionized the
world. Men began to study the laws of electricity and to
apply them.

Jesus Christ Revealed and Applied the Laws of the Spirit

Jesus Christ came to reveal the laws of the Spirit and
to apply them. In the heart of God there is a dynamic, a
power which is great enough to save every man in the
world, to heal every sick person in the world—to heal
them of anything, of any degree of sin or any degree of
sickness, to raise the dead, bless God. This is my conception of what went on in the mind of the Son of God:
"To the extent that I can uncover the minds of men, so
that they can see this and appropriate it for their benefit,
I can save the world." Any way, that is what He proceeded to work out. So through His life, through His
death, through His resurrection from the dead, step by
step, He went to the throne of God and presented Himself and received from the Father the Gift of the Holy
Ghost. Then He said, "Here it is," and proceeded to bless
the world with it. Acts 2. And ever since He has been
pouring it out upon the world, upon whosoever would
receive it. Bless God!

The Power of God's Spirit will do for you what it has
done for any one else in the world. But, beloved, you must
come to God with earnestness and sincerity and faith and
lay hold of it. Do you suppose that Benjamin Franklin
would have discovered electricity if he had not believed
there was electricity? You will not get any healing from
heaven if you do not believe that there is any for you.
You will never get it applied to your body, or your soul
or spirit so it will do you any good, until you lay hold of
it intelligently and receive it.

That is why we have people testify to what God has
done, and try to tell one another of God's action in their

lives, until your soul comes into the intelligence of the faith, and you see that the redemption of Jesus Christ was not a mythical matter, but an actual scientific fact. So Christ was not a sentimental dreamer. He had His finger on the keys of the universe. He knew the treasure stored in the soul of the eternal God. He said, "I must bring this to mankind. They must see, feel, experience it. It must take hold of them and change them and revolutionize them." Bless God!

Sitting before me is a man who was healed of rupture. The hernia would leave him in an agony of hell, and he sometimes worked all night to get the organs back in place. He suffered torture for seventeen years. Then one night some friends took him to a cottage meeting. A few saints gathered around and put their hands on him, and the fire of God, that blessing Jesus died for, that Jesus received from the soul of the Father, came down on his soul and body and he got up with his rupture healed. It's a wonderful salvation isn't it?

Chapter VIII

NAAMAN AND THE MAN OF GOD

(At the beginning of the service Dr. Lake called a young lady to the platform by the name of Celia Prentice. She had been healed of a short leg.)

Mr. Lake then spoke:

This girl is seventeen years old now. She was born paralyzed from the waist down. When nine years old, a surgeon made a lot of steel braces, by which she was able to brace herself and stand and walk with crutches. The left leg was two inches shorter from birth. She came for prayer and in ten days from the time she was first ministered to, the leg had grown to normal length. She wore a shoe with a two inch sole and a peculiar upper.

In this case there was a creative action. The leg two inches short becomes normal by the touch of God. How marvelously this illustrates the power of God in the souls of men. People say, "I was born with this weakness, or that weakness." Or "I have this mental tendency, or that mental tendency," just as if they should remain that way forever; as if there were no God; as if His business were not to restore their personality, body, soul, and spirit, and bring them into the likeness of Jesus Christ the Perfect Man.

You see instant healings and gradual healings, just as you see instant conversions and those who have to be gradually enlightened. How many of you knew all about the fullness of Christ's salvation when you were converted? How many have lived without making any progress since the Lord forgave you? If I were going to quarrel with the church at large, it would be because they perpetuate infancy. People are born of God, and then remain babes. That is not God's ideal.

I have preached the Gospel about thirty-four years,

64

and about nine of those years without knowing Christ as the Healer. Consequently, life has had some experiences and particularly along the line of Divine healing and the Baptism of the Holy Ghost, which have characterized my ministry. Hence, I speak from experience.

The Scripture Lesson

"Now Naaman, captain of the host of the king of Syria, was a great man with his master, and honorable, because by him the Lord had given deliverance unto Syria: he was also a mighty man in valour, but he was a leper." 2 Kings 5.

Naaman was your General Pershing, your General Haig, your Foch or Hindenburg. He was a conqueror and had delivered Syria from the bondage of the nations about them. He was a mighty man in valour but he was a leper. This tells us a sad story. Then through the testimony of a brave little maid, his master learned about the fact of the power of God to heal in the land of Israel.

The king of Syria sent Naaman to the king of Israel. That king had no power to heal a leper. Then Elisha came to the latter's rescue, saying, "Let him come now to me, and he shall know that there is a prophet in Israel."

I want to touch a phase of Divine healing that I feel is neglected. I feel that the Lord is misrepresented. I feel that many Divine healing teachers have not grown up into the stature in Christ where they take the position that the Lord ascribes to them in the Word of God. There is a continual effort to shift all the responsibility on the other party. And when they cannot do this successfully, they try to throw it back on God. Don't you know that this is the attitude to which unbelief and lack of faith have brought the church?

In the early church the normal method was to call for the elders of the church. They would anoint with oil and the prayer of faith would save the sick. The person would be healed, and if he had committed sin, it would be forgiven him. When the early Christians anointed, they prayed the prayer of faith. It was figurative that right there and then the benefits and powers of the Cross of Jesus Christ were made available to the soul, and by the actual touch of the oil, represent the living Spirit of God as thus present to perform the healing.

After awhile the church backslid, then traded away the gifts of God, sold the gift of the Holy Ghost, drifted into formality, came up through a thousand years of the Dark Ages, getting darker and darker, until when Martin Luther came, the Christian world had lost consciousness of the truth of salvation by faith. The church had substituted a human creation called "penance."

That was the only conception of salvation left. Martin Luther's whole message was, "The just shall live by faith." It was a revelation of God. Salvation not by penances, but by faith in the living Son of God. One cannot imagine how it was possible for the church to have drifted away into such a condition. It shows how far the church has drifted from the pure ideal of the Lord Jesus Christ and apostolic times. We have a long road to come back. We are only infants. The greatest of spiritual men are but infants prattling around on the shores of the great sea of eternal light, life and power, compared to what the early church actually possessed and revealed.

Well, when they lost faith they had to substitute something else. The elders and the priests continued to pray for the sick, but they had no faith in their souls and the individual died. They prayed for another and he died. Imagine the condition of the church and the elders after once having been anointed with the glory and the power of God. Now the power had departed, but still the elder goes through the ceremony. He anoints with oil, and he prays but nothing happens. So the church came to the relief of such, and they took that beautiful ceremony of the anointing with oil and the prayer of faith, and they changed it into what is known as "the sacrament of extreme unction." They took away the conception of healing and made it a ceremony of consolation for the dying.

Beloved the Protestant Church was born in no greater faith than that. The Protestant Church under Martin Luther was born with a faith for the salvation of men's souls, but there they put up the bars. Philip Melanchthon is a lonely example of healing, more through Luther's despair than his faith.

In the life of Wesley, advance was made. Wesley records two hundred and forty cases of healing in his writings, of every class of disease. He regarded these deliverances apparently as a triumph of human faith, emphasizing the thought that man's extremity was God's opportunity.

That is not the true basis of healing. It is not because a man is in need. It is because it is the Divine purpose of Jesus Christ to redeem mankind from all sin and the consequences of sin. Sickness being the consequence of sin, and death being the consequence of sin, are ascribed by the Lord to the devil. Death was not the servant of God, but an enemy, and Jesus Christ is going to destroy death. "The last enemy that shall be destroyed is death." Bless God, that is the Divine consummation. Then sinlessness, sicklessness and deathlessness shall be established in the world. "No man shall say, know the Lord, for they all shall know him from the least to the greatest."

And when sickness is gone, there will be no more drugs and operations. No more rattling of clods on coffin lids, for, "Death is swallowed up in victory." That is why Jesus Christ died. There was never any other standard for the church of Jesus Christ than that of dominion over sickness. Let us keep the standard high, where Jesus placed it. I want you to keep that fact forever clear, that the purpose of Christ's redemption is sinlessness, sicklessness and ultimately deathlessness. Bless God, that is His ideal for man. A man to be as perfect as Jesus Christ was perfect. Matt. 5:48. We may never get one half or one quarter of the way toward the ideal. But never try to degrade God's purpose and bring it down to your level. But by the Grace of God put the standard up there where Jesus put it, and then get as near it as you can.

After the church lost faith in God, they began to lie about God. They came to a man's bedside and said, "Your sickness is the Will of God." Well, it is the work of the devil, and in the ultimate sense every death that ever took place was the work of the devil. Even at the crucifixion Jesus said, "This is your hour, and the power of darkness." Christ died in substitutionary consequence of the law of sin, and not in consequence of the law of life. When Jesus Christ finally puts His mighty power into action, and brings the abolition of death into manifestation, sin, sickness, and death are done forever.

Old Job started an error about the Will of God. A cyclone came from the wilderness and took the lives of his sons. He then said, "The Lord gave, and the Lord hath taken away, blessed be the name of the Lord." Only in the permissive sense is such a statement true. The Scriptures distinctly show that it was Satan who went forth from the presence of the Lord and caused these things to happen. But the world has perpetuated that lie, and many a preacher uses it in the burial service, and tries to stamp it on the impressionable mind of man.

My surprise is not that there are so few healed, but that anybody, under the circumstances, is healed. For 1400 years men have erred about the Will of God, until the world is almost infidel as the result of it.

Occasions When God Demands Action Instead of Prayer

Moses came down to the Red Sea. The mountains were impassable on the right hand and on the left. Pharaoh's armies were following him down the Pass. He had two million men, women, and children on his hands. The Red Sea was in front of him. When he got to the Red Sea he stopped and did just what you do, and everyone else tries to do when they get into a hard place—back up and begin to pray. So instead of walking into the water and stretching out his rod, he backed up and began to pray. And the Lord went after him. That is one occasion when the Lord rebuked a man for praying. So many try to crawl out by praying. And the Lord said to Moses:

"Wherefore criest thou unto me? Speak unto the children of Israel, that they go forward: But lift up thy rod, and stretch out thine hand over the sea, and divide it." Exod. 14:15, 16.

In other words, "Moses *you* divide it." Our prayer is, "Now Lord, you come and heal this man." Don't you see the mistake? It was not the way that Peter healed. Peter met the lame man and said, "Silver and gold have I none; but such as I have give I thee: In the name of Jesus Christ of Nazareth rise up and walk." Acts 3:6. Bless God, Peter had something to give. It was God's power.

The Christian's Responsibility

God Almighty laid the responsibility on the individual who knows God, not on the other fellow. A young man came to me with tuberculosis. He said, "Mr. Lake, I am a tubercular man. I have been passed up by the doctors. I have heard that people were healed here but I have no faith." I answered, "Well dear boy, if you haven't I have. I know God. I am a child of God." The Christian is the one who ought to have faith. This was the attitude of the

early church. "Go and heal them," said Jesus. And they
went and healed them. This young man is now one of
our preachers.

Do not throw the responsibility entirely on the other
person. If he has no faith, give him some. Instruct him,
give him the Word of God. Jesus ministered the faith
of God in His teaching services so that people were able
to receive healing. The Spirit of God ministered by Jesus
was effective to produce faith in the souls of men and
heal them too. Healing for the body, soul, and spirit.

Queen Wilhelmina of Holland entered the state of
motherhood six times, but was never able to carry the
child to maturity. All the science of Europe could not
bring the child to birth. There was a dear lady in our
congregation in South Africa who had formerly been a
nurse to Queen Wilhelmina. Her son was marvelously
healed when dying of African fever, when he had been
unconscious for six weeks.

Being a friend of the queen, she wrote the story of her
son's healing, and after some correspondence we received
a written request that we pray God that she might be a
real mother. I brought her letter before the congregation
one Sunday night, and the congregation went down to
prayer. And before I arose from my knees, I turned
around and said, "All right mother, you write and tell
the queen, God has heard our prayer; she will bear a
child." Less than a year later the child was born, the
present Princess Julianna of Holland. Kings and queens
are only men and women. They need the redemption of
Jesus and are a mighty poor article without it. "And it
was so, when Elisha the man of God had heard that the
king of Israel had rent his clothes, that he sent unto the
king, saying . . . let him come now to me, and he shall
know that there is a prophet in Israel."

Don't you know that more and more I feel that we
preachers have too apologetic an attitude. We sort of

apologize to the world. We have so many niceties that we are afraid to state that we are men of God. We have all sorts of cunning little ways, and we call them niceties. There is not the realization of the dignity and responsibility that should be evident in the man of God. Actually we are sidestepping. There is a better place of Christian boldness than that, and before we can take the world for Jesus Christ, we will assume a different attitude toward sin, and darkness, and hell.

"So Naaman came with his horses and with his chariot, and stood at the door of the house of Elisha. And Elisha sent a messenger unto him, saying, Go and wash in Jordan seven times, and thy flesh shall come again to thee, and thou shalt be clean. But Naaman was wroth, and went away and said, . . . Are not the Abana and Pharpar, rivers of Damascus, better than all the rivers of Israel? may I not wash in them, and be clean?"

2 Kings 5:9-12.

It was not the waters of Jordan that would make him clean. It was obedience to Almighty God. People have not learned that lesson very well. A man came in not long ago, and as I prayed I said, "You come in every day for the next thirty days, and if you do you will be well." So he came for a week and then got lazy and did not come again. In about two months he returned again, and I said, "When you get ready to obey God, I will pray for you again. I told you to come every day for thirty days." He said, "I came for eight days." Well, God let that fellow come for twenty-nine days. His healing was complete on the twenty-ninth day. But a lot of other things happened before that. He got under conviction for sin and found that there was a God in heaven, and there was something else in life beside getting a well body. God needs some time to get things worked out in our souls.

The most unsatisfactory character of healings are our instant healings. In most cases you have a healed baby

on your hands, and you have to run around with a nurs-
ing bottle for a year or two to get them straightened out
and going on with God strong and clear.

Faith is not a spasmodic impulse. It is the attitude of
the soul. It is the set of your spirit. There is a verse that
I like very much:

> "One ship goes east another west,
>   By the self same gale that blows.
>   'Tis not the gale, but the set of the sail
>   That determines which way it goes."

You set your soul toward God, knowing that the Blood
of Jesus Christ hath made provision for your redemption
from sin and sickness, and pursue it until you find it.

In our African work we have a native man by the
name of Edward Lion. When he first came to us he was a
raw Zulu heathen, and wore a goat skin apron eight
inches square, as his sole raiment. He was converted,
and about a year and a half afterward was baptized in the
Holy Ghost. On Christmas Eve of 1912 in Basutoland,
South Africa, we served the Lord's supper to seventy-five
lepers healed under that man's ministry.

*"And his servants came near ... and said, My father,
if the prophet had bid thee do some great thing, wouldst
thou not have done it? how much rather then, when he
saith to thee, Wash and be clean? Then went he down
and dipped himself seven times in Jordan, according to
the saying of the man of God: and his flesh came again
like unto the flesh of a little child, and he was clean."*

I was conducting a Divine healing meeting in Wak-
erstrom, South Africa, when they brought in sixty-five
sick people. We stood them in line and prayed for them
one by one as they went by. Sixty out of the sixty-five
were healed. Five were not healed. I wanted to inter-
view these five, so we took them one at a time. I asked,
"What is the difficulty? Is there any reason that you

know of that you were not healed?" One man confessed
to adultery, and when he repented to God we prayed
again, and he was instantly healed. A woman confessed
to being a persistent thief. We charged her and accepted
her pledge to God that she would go and confess and make
restitution as far as was possible. She was healed the moment that she made that confession and agreement with
God.

"If our hearts condemn us not, then have we confidence toward God." You do not have to pump faith into a
man when his sin is taken away and his disobedience is
gone, bless God. Then the pathway is made clear. We
took four hours to deal with those five people, but I had
the gratification of writing in my diary: "We prayed for
sixty-five people and every one was healed."

We do not know much about the Gifts of the Spirit
yet. During the life of my late wife, she had the Gift of
Discernment in a greater degree than I did. As I prayed
for people, if they were not healed, I passed them on into
another room; and when the crowd was off my hands, I
would call my wife in. She would lay her hands on an
individual and say, "At such and such a time you committed a sin." Probably to another she would say, "The
Lord shows me that the particular difficulty is so and so."
And when they got the matter settled with God, we would
pray again, and the Lord healed them.

Beloved, the mere fact of the presence of the Gifts of
Healing and the Baptism of the Holy Ghost is not evidence of God's full purposes. The ministry of the Holy
Ghost is set forth in the nine gifts of the Holy Ghost.
And we have been looking for a church that has it entirely. I am glad that we can see that since the coming
of the blessed Baptism of the Holy Ghost all these things
are becoming real to the Christian church. For the first
fifteen years of my ministry I was considered as an insane

man, a fanatic, because of the fact that God had revealed
the ministry of healing and used me in that ministry.

Now a whole lot of you are like a dear woman who
has been coming here. She came the other day and said,
"Mr. Lake, I have been prayed for three times and I do
not think that I am any better." I answered, "I do not
think that you will ever be any better until something
happens in your life. You came with the thought of experimenting with God, and if you are not healed you
could go and be operated on. Now if your consecration
to God does not mean any more to you than that, you are
only playing with God. God wants you to cut clear."

Consecration means something. Jesus Christ went
down to the Jordan and gave His Body, Soul and Spirit
forever to God. Jesus gave the one and perfect pattern for
Christian consecration for all time. He gave His Body,
Soul and Spirit to God once and forever and then lived it.

That is the reason that the day I invited Jesus Christ
to come into my heart and become my physician, I have
trusted no other since. We represent the kingdom of
heaven and the living God, and to reveal them to mankind is what we live for, and stand for, and are ready to
die for. Bless God.

Chapter IX

CONSECRATION, TESTING, POWER, VICTORY

I wish we could follow the Lord Jesus today in the steps of His life, and the anticipation of His victory. You know we have our eyes so fixed on the fact that Jesus was the Son of God, therefore of course Divine, that we lose sight of the fact that He was also a Man just like other men. That all the soul battles that any man has to meet, Jesus had to meet. It is the realization of this fact that creates such fellowship. It seems to me that the sin of modern Christianity has been the isolation of Jesus into a class by Himself. Then Christians proceed to excuse themselves all along the line on the ground that Jesus was God. Jesus did this because He was God. Jesus had victory because He was God. Jesus healed because He was God.

No, beloved, Jesus was just as much a Man as you and I. Jesus met every challenge of the soul, just as you and I have to meet it. But Jesus willed to do God's Will and to know God's Will.

How to Enter the Will of God—Two Phases

There are two phases of entering into the Will of God. The first is the surrender of our Will to do the Will of God. Most people's conception of doing the Will of God is to become a non-entity. Now it is not God's ideal for you to have to be pushed around like a machine, or moved like a mechanism. The other, is recognizing yourself as God's son and man's servant. I think the most wonderful exhibition of this truth that God can give us, is in the fact that He gives us the Holy Ghost to use for God.

For instance the Lord says, "They shall lay hands on

the sick, and they shall recover." But if you do not lay
your hands upon anyone they will not be healed. However, if you have faith to believe you have the Holy
Spirit to be used by Him and for Him, your hands and
heart will be ready. It is a sad thing to me that God had
to go out on a special mission and hunt a soul up and
wrestle with him in order to get him to do something for
God.

There used to be a Bible School in Ohio where they
waited in continuous prayer meeting for nine months for
the Gifts of the Holy Ghost. I said to them, "It seems to
me if you stay around for ten years and nine months you
will miss the Gifts of the Holy Ghost. But if you take
off your coat and go out and use what God has given you
to bless others, He will give you more."

Jesus First Dedicates Himself

Jesus first dedicated Himself. That is the secret of His
life. He dedicated Himself not to do His will, but to do
the Will of God. That is what His baptism at Jordan
meant. Jesus dedicated Himself to God, Body, Soul and
Spirit. How many of you have dedicated body, soul and
spirit to God? (Many hands raised.) Now all those who
took a dose of pills during the last two or three months,
put your hands up. (No response.) Pill swallowers do
not like to put their hands up.

I want you to see that the dedication of your body,
soul and spirit means something. It means you have
taken yourself out of the hands of man and out of the
hands of the devil, and are over in God's way and God's
will forever. Suppose you have a difficulty in your spirit.
Where do you go for relief? You might go over and hang
around those Spiritualists, but that would not be God's
way. That is a way a lot of poor folks do.

We have a neighbor who has been a very ardent Spir-
itualist. One day he rode to town with me, and he told

me how fascinated he was. Last week he ran off with another fellow's wife. I have this much to say on that line. I have watched the progress and process of Spiritualism for years, and it usually ends that way. The tendency is downward, not upward, into selfishness and sensuality.

No, when we have a difficulty in our spirit, we go to the Father of spirits. When we have a difficulty in our soul, we do not go to the spirit of the world. We go to the Lord. When we have a difficulty in our body, to whom do we go? Most Christians go to the world, flesh and the devil. The trouble is in our consecration. We have not a real vision of the Christian's consecration and what constitutes it.

The Lord provided a salvation for the spirit, a salvation for the soul, and a salvation for the body. The violator is not just a weak Christian, but he is a sinner. He is a sinner against the Will of God and against the spirit of Christian consecration, for the Christian's consecration demands a separation unto Jesus Christ of all that Christ separated unto God the Father. That was the consecration of the early Christians. The primitive church regarded the individual who took the world's way of pills and medicine as having departed from the way of Jesus, and they were dealt with in love and disciplined just the same as if they had stolen a horse or committed some other sin. They were treated as having sinned and needing restoration to God.

You say, "That is very drastic." It may be, but it is very true. That is the law of God. It is not only the law of God, but is "the law of the spirit of life in Christ Jesus." Do you suppose if you go up to heaven you will find a lot of folks who are full of pills, headache tablets, or nux vomica?

One of the prescriptions for healing in the Talmud is to repeat the Ninety-first Psalm seven times a day. Well, if a man repeated the Ninety-first Psalm seven

times a day, he would not keep it up long before the
spirit of faith in the Almighty God got into his soul. That
was good medicine for the soul, and good medicine for
the body also.

The Extent of Jesus' Dedication

If you are questioning the extent to which Jesus
dedicated Himself, you can see the fulness of it in the
story of His temptation in the wilderness. Satan tempted
Him in the three departments of His life. First in the
physical. Second in the psychological. Third in the spiritual. First he tempted Him to turn the stones into bread
for the satisfaction of His physical needs. Then he
tempted Him to get the acclaim of the multitude. A lot
of preachers are doing that still. Satan set Him on the
pinnacle of the temple, told Him to cast Himself down.
A psychological temptation in the realm of the soul.

The third was a spiritual temptation. Satan took
Him up into an exceeding high mountain, and showed
Him all the kingdoms of the world and the glory of
them, and said, "All these things will I give thee, if thou
wilt fall down and worship me." By a spiritual flash, one
of the marvels of the spirit, Jesus is permitted to view all
the kingdoms of the world and the glory of them in a moment of time. He did not just let His imagination travel
out, but He saw them in their magnificence, and wonder
and glory. And Satan said, "All these things will I give
thee, if thou wilt fall down and worship me."

You see His body had been dedicated, and His soul
likewise to God, not to anybody else. He was utterly
given up to God. I was talking with Mrs. Lake yesterday
while we were out driving. I said, "Florence, the greatest
sense of freedom that I ever experienced and the happiest
days that I ever lived were after I had given away all I
had." The night I preached my first sermon in the fulness of this gospel, I purposely gave away the last five

dollars I had, to a widow. I just wanted to get rid of it. It was a wonderful thing to get the weights all off your soul.

Beloved what are the difficulties that you are struggling over? What is it that is keeping your soul down? Why bless you, in most cases it is a mere trifle. So when I did not have a cent, then the Lord took me to Africa. I do not believe that He would have ever told me to go if I had not obeyed Him. God said, "You are going to Africa," and I was totally broke. Most of you know the story of how I got there. We had a beautiful home in Africa. It was unusual in that it was built of wood. It was not as nice as our former woodshed in this country, but we were never so happy as we were there. The roof was of galvanized iron. I slept in the attic. Under that African sun in the summer time, it was seven times hotter than the Babylonian furnace, and just as soon as the sun set it was cooler than a refrigerator. But I slept in that attic and got some of the most beautiful things from God, and it was there that many of the truths I preach to you today were revealed to me.

First dedicate yourself to God. I wonder if you have done it? You old church people who have been taking pills and every other old thing, have you dedicated yourself to God? Get through with it all and give your body to the Lord. Make Jesus Christ your Physician forever; take Him as your only remedy.

The Result of Dedication

The result of that dedication was that you could not have kept Jesus from the Baptism of the Holy Ghost. God has been waiting for a long time for folks to do that. My, the heart of God responds to that sort of consecration. When Jesus stood by the waters of Jordan and made that consecration, something took place in the soul of the Father and the flood-tide of heaven's glory came down—

appearing as a Dove resting upon Christ. At least it looked to John as if a Dove rested upon Him. The Spirit did not come in little dribbles. "He giveth not the Spirit by measure unto Him." It came down from heaven in fullness, out of the heart of God.

First, Jesus dedicated His all to the Father. The result was that the Holy Ghost descended upon Him and Jesus was filled with the Spirit. When you get filled with the Spirit, you will have something coming to you that is not all shouts and glory and happiness. Right away Satan got on the track of Jesus. He will get on yours too, if you make that sort of consecration. Somebody is filled with the Spirit and Satan knows there is going to be trouble for him. He must get on the job and side track that individual if he can.

So Jesus was led into the wilderness; not by the devil but by the Holy Ghost. Isn't that a strange thing that the Holy Ghost led Him into the wilderness? What for? To meet the devil. Why? To try Him whether He was going to be an overcomer or not; to see whether He meant what He said at the Jordan. The devil said, "Did You mean the consecration that You made? Did You mean when You gave Your Body and Soul to the Lord at the Jordan, that it was forever?"

Most folks mean their consecration on the day they are baptized, and then forget it the first time that the devil appears, or they get a pain in the stomach. It was a forever business with the Lord Jesus. Get that forever thing into your soul and spirit. There never was a time in history, when the world needed a demonstration that the Lord could keep people forever, under every condition, as much as it does today.

Jesus had thus dedicated His Body, Soul and Spirit to God forever, and Satan tried Him to the finish on each point. A woman recently saved was afterward in despair. Everything had gone wrong from the time that she was converted. She was married to a wretch of a man. He told her if she were going to be a Christian he was through, and away he went. The next thing she knew her best friend went insane. Then her mother gave her heart to God, and she had not been a Christian for a week before her husband came home and said, "What has happened to you?" She told him that she had found God. He said, "Goodbye!" and that was the last they saw of him. Then she had her mother and the insane friend to care for. She was distracted and driven.

One day in the agony of her despair, she was ready to throw up her hands. She said, "O God, after all I have experienced there is nothing else for me to do. I am going back into the world." About that time the Spirit said to me, "Go over to Salmon Street right away." I drove over and met her. As she came down the steps I reached out my hand and asked, as I saw the cloud on her face, "Well, how is it?" She replied, "Don't mention it. It is hell! Is this what folks get for being Christians?" I said, "I do not know dear sister, but one thing is dead sure, when you get through this you will know whether you are a Christian or not." Then I urged, "Dear little woman, this is not the time to throw up your hands in the midst of the battle. Any fool can do that. You win this battle, and then go and backslide." She answered, "All right, I will stick to this battle for two weeks." I said, "That is a bargain."

At the end of the two weeks I said, "Now dear sister, you go and backslide." She smiled and said, "I don't think so." The little insane friend was healed. The dear old mother was healed. Some friends discovered what was going on and filled their house with the sick, and they were healed. It pays to go through.

First Jesus dedicated all His Being, Body, Soul and Spirit to God the Father. Next, the Holy Ghost from heaven came upon Him. He entered the temptation *filled* with the Spirit. He returned from the battle in the *power* of the Spirit.

I prayed for the Baptism of the Holy Ghost for nine months, and if a man ever prayed honestly and sincerely in the faith, I did. Finally one day I was ready to throw up my hands and quit. I said, "Lord, it may be for others, but it is not for me. You just cannot give it to me." I did not blame God.

One night a gentleman by the name of Pierce said, "Mr. Lake, I have been wishing for a long time you would come over and we would spend a night in prayer together. We have been praying for the Baptism for a whole year and there is not one of us baptized yet. Brother, I do not believe that you are either, so we can pray for one another." I was so hungry to pray, so I went with all the intentions of praying for the rest, but I had not been praying five minutes until the light of God began to shine around me. I found myself in a center of an arc of light ten feet in diameter—the whitest light in all the universe. So white! O how it spoke of purity. The remembrance of that whiteness, that wonderful whiteness, has been the ideal that has stood before my soul, of the purity of the nature of God ever since.

A Voice Spoke Out of the Vision of Light

Then a Voice began to talk to me out of that light. There was no form. And the Voice began to remind me of this incident and that incident of disobedience to my parents, from a child; of my obstinacy, and dozens of instances when God brought me up to the line of absolutely putting my body, soul and spirit upon the altar forever. I had my body upon the altar for ten years, and I had been a minister of the Gospel. But when the Lord comes, He opens to the soul the depths that have never been touched in your life. Do you know that after I was baptized in the Holy Ghost, things opened up in the depths of my nature that had remained untouched all my life, and that which was shadowy, distant, and hazy became real. God got up close and let His light shine into me. A short time after, I received the Holy Ghost.

You have been sticking away off in the background. You have been following Him a week or two, and then back off. Beloved, you will never get anywhere that way. God has a hard time jarring us loose, and getting us out where we will step out on God and stand.

Jesus went through that awful testing. Supposing He had weakened? Supposing He had gone off and bought a box of pills? He would have been a blemished Lamb. Just once would have rendered His consecration valueless. When He went into the Wilderness He HAD THE SPIRIT, but after He went through the testing, the SPIRIT HAD HIM. Do you get it? A lot of folks have the Spirit of God. Every child of God has the Spirit in a degree, but after they have gone through with God the Spirit has them.

The Result of the Wilderness Testing

When He came out of the wilderness in the Power of the Spirit, when the Holy Ghost had Him, Body, Soul and Spirit, every fibre of Him, He was ready to go out and demonstrate what Christianity is. We read:

"And Jesus went about all Galilee, teaching in their synagogues, and preaching the gospel of the kingdom, and healing all manner of sickness... among the people." Matt. 4:23.

Everybody wants to jump in and preach, but bless God, when we are willing to go through with Jesus in that "getting ready" process, then it will be with effectiveness, it will be with power, it will be with the love of God.

Charles Parham was preaching in the state of Kansas. An old farmer was very interested, and was all the time saying, "O, I wish the Lord would take all my farms and my cattle and all my possessions and let me preach the Gospel." So one night Parham got down to pray and he prayed, "Lord God in heaven, send a pestilence and kill all the cattle; let the lightnings come and burn up the sheep." And the man got up with a start, and said, "What are you praying that way for?" Parham said, "Well, didn't you mean what you said?"

God bless you, we do not mean half of what we pray. But it finally dawned on that fellow's soul what a real consecration was, and one day he went out and used the finances in the Gospel of Jesus Christ to get men's souls saved. He backed a dozen missionary boards. Years afterward I was walking down the street of Johannesburg, South Africa, when a street car came along and something said to jump on. The first fellow I saw was this chap. He told me he had just taken a missionary party up to the Congo and settled them, and he remarked, "The work we planted there is going on until Jesus comes and never stop." Wouldn't you like to plant something that would go on until Jesus comes, that would bless mankind?

One night in 1909 I was preaching in Los Angeles, and in the course of my address I made the statement that I was located where conditions were such that I would guarantee a soul for every cent invested. I came on to Portland. I had gathered a party of eight that I wanted to take back to Africa. I had money enough for my own personal expenses but not enough for them. One night I knelt by my bed and prayed, "Lord, I have labored these six months and these eight people are ready to go back with me, and I believe every one of them is truly called of God. I haven't a cent to take them. Now it's up to You." I got into bed feeling that I had been heard.

Four or five nights afterward, the night before my meeting closed, I came in about 2 a.m. and found a letter from George B. Studd. It read, "Lake, there has been a windfall in your favor today. A friend of yours came in and asked that her identity be not revealed, and she said, 'This is for Lake, of South Africa.' She left a draft for $3,000.00. I have five dollars of my own I am putting with it."

I took my party back to Africa. I felt that money was a challenge to the thing that I had said, that I would present a saved soul for every cent invested. That would mean 300,000 saved. I want to tell you that there are 50,000 now. How many souls will that $3,000.00 produce if the Lord tarries for 50 years more?

God showed me the value of souls. I was manager of agents for a life insurance company. I received 80% flat on the first premiums. Twenty or thirty minutes with a man might mean a commission of many hundreds of dollars. But God baptized me in the Holy Ghost, and I went back to my office at the end of thirty days, and I never had such a time to talk insurance to a man. The Holy Ghost kept saying "How about his soul?" After a little bit I had to stop and say, "Brother, are you a Christian? If not kneel down." I would kneel down and start to pray, and I saw them come to God every day for six months. But O, I forgot about the insurance and the company was paying me to get insurance. I said, "This has gotten to be such a battle, it is either God and souls now or it is business." I fought that for six months. At the end, the Lord won.

First give yourself to God, body, soul and spirit. That will take your money and everything else with it. Bless God! It did for Jesus and it did for me. "The foxes have holes, and the birds of the air have nests, but the son of man hath not where to lay his head," said Jesus.

When on the African mission fields, my wife, seven children, and I sat down an hundred times when we did not have a thing but corn meal mush, and sometimes did not have salt to put on it, yet I preached three or four times a day, and ministered to the sick continuously. My heart is hungry for it now. I would say, "Goodbye to your pumpkin pie and everything else," and go back to mush, if I could have the same victory for Jesus Christ.

Chapter X

THE BRAZEN SERPENT

The healing of the Israelites in the Wilderness at the time that Moses lifted up the Brazen Serpent, is one of the familiar lessons to most Bible students. Israel had a marvelous experience of deliverance and great conquest over Arad, king of the Canaanites, at which time God had utterly delivered them into her hands. "And Israel vowed a vow unto the Lord, and said, If thou wilt indeed deliver this people into my hand, then I will utterly destroy their cities. And the Lord hearkened to the voice of Israel, and delivered up the Canaanites." Nu. 21:2, 3.

But Israel soon forgot her vow. Some folks forget all about God so soon. Jesus said, concerning the lepers which were healed and only one returned to give God the glory, "Were there not ten cleansed? Where are the nine?" So we read in the fifth verse that "the people spake against God, and against Moses." Moses had asked to pass through the land of the Edomites, promising that they would touch nothing in their vineyards nor drink the water of their wells. But Edom said "Thou shalt not pass by me, lest I come out against thee with the sword." Nu. 20:18. So the people were compelled to compass the land of Edom. This was the reason that the people complained against God and against Moses.

You can almost hear the Children of Israel as they groaned. "Wherefore have you brought us up out of Egypt to die in the wilderness?" It sounds like some Christians. Unless they are whooping it up on top of the house, they are away down in the valley, where it is terribly dark and sad. Israel had had a great triumph, but now she had been led through a hard way and she began complaining: "For there is no bread, neither is there any water; and our soul loatheth this light bread." The light bread was the Manna.

Well, something happened. "And the Lord sent fiery serpents among the people, and they bit the people; and much people of Israel died." Verse 6. Dr. Young's translation makes that read in the permissive sense. "And the Lord PERMITTED fiery serpents to come among the people." The Lord had been protecting them and keeping the fiery serpents off all of the time, but they did not know it. So the Lord just let the serpents come among them. When did you have your last growl, or an awful spell of the blue devils? There is a place where the Christian soul gets through with all that kind of stuff.

Confession Then a Remedy Provided

"*Therefore the people came to Moses, and said, We have sinned, for we have spoken against the Lord, and against thee; pray unto the Lord, that he will take away the serpents from us. And Moses prayed for the people.*" Vs. 7.

Real confession should always precede your prayer for healing. CONFESS your sin, then pray. It was a good thing Moses had grown up a little in God. Think of a man with over two million to growl at him. There is a place where the soul grows up. Moses prayed for the Children of Israel, and God gave him a remedy:

"*And the Lord said unto Moses, Make thee a fiery serpent, and set it upon a pole: and it shall come to pass, that every one that is bitten, when he looketh upon it, shall live.*" Vs. 8.

God was directing their minds back to the original Covenant. How many of you know what the first Covenant was that God made with man? God said to the serpent, "I will put enmity between thee and the woman, and between thy seed and her seed; it shall bruise thy head, and thou shalt bruise his heel." Gen. 3:15. That first Covenant promised a Serpent Bruiser. He made that Covenant with the whole race. It is one of our universal Covenants, and we have the right to look back there and expect the fulfillment of the Promise.

The Power of God's Promises

One of our ministers was limited in words and ability to express his thoughts, but he had a wonderful ministry of healing. One day I went with him to make his calls. After the first call I said, "I have not come to pray, you just go ahead and pray yourself. I am going to keep still." And when he began to pray I saw what the secret of that man's prayer was. It was the power of the promise. "God, You said it," and he would quote another Promise. The result was that he not only inspired faith in his own soul, but also the faith of God in the individual that needed the blessing.

So in this instance God took the eye of the whole nation, and turned it back to the first Promise of the Eternal God. Do you remember when Jesus wanted a precedent on which to establish His teaching on the subject of marriage and divorce? He did not go back to Moses but clear back to Eden. "Therefore shall a man leave his father and his mother, and shall cleave unto his wife: and they shall be one flesh."

Taking the Sting Out of the Serpent

There is another lesson I want you to see. That is, Jesus taking the sting out of the serpent. God promised that Christ would bruise the serpent's head, but in the process of bruising, "he shall bruise thy heel." That is, in the bruising of the serpent's head, Jesus Christ would be bruised in the effort. The bruising of the heel took place when Jesus Christ died on the Cross. But in the bruising of the heel, the head of the serpent was to be crushed forever. The serpent and all he stands for is to be blotted from the world. The serpent represented the thing cursed of God.

Sin will curse anything. The sin of the world made Jesus Himself the cursed thing, and as the accursed and the criminal, He was nailed to the Cross, having taken on Himself our curse and criminality. "Being made a curse for us: for it is written, Cursed is everyone that hangeth on a tree." That was the manner in which Jesus took the sting out of the serpent. And Paul goes on to elucidate this matter, and breaks out with great joy: "O death where is thy sting? O grave, where is thy victory?" 1 Cor. 15:55. The sting of death is sin, but Christ having come, sin was abolished and the sting taken away.

I think among all the wonderful symbols of the Word of God none stands out emphasizing more powerfully the conquest of Jesus Christ than this symbol of the serpent, which had bitten and cursed Israel, and then God held up before the people, saying, "Now look upon it, and you will live." Why? Because of the power of the PROMISE, because of the Covenant, because of the bruising, and because He became a curse for us. Blessed be God forever and ever!

Utter Defeat of the Devil

The New Testament reveals to us the utterness of the serpent's defeat. The Word says, "Resist the devil and he will flee from you." He has become to the anointed soul, the symbol of defeat. "He (Jesus) came to destroy the devil." That is His purpose, "forasmuch then as the children are partakers of flesh and blood, he also himself likewise took part of the same; that through death he might destroy him that had the power of death, that is, the devil." Heb. 2:14.

My, how the Word of God reveals, not only Jesus Christ's own triumph over the devil and darkness, but the triumph of the Christian who enters into oneness with Christ. Bless God, the final consummation is revealed to us by the Apostle John in Rev. 1:18, when Jesus in exaltation of His glory stood forth declaring, "I am he that liveth, and was dead; and, behold, I am alive forevermore, Amen; and have the keys of hell and of death." Yes sir, the keys of darkness were delivered into the hands of the Son of God; He has them. He paid for them at the Cross. That is the principle Jesus laid down when He said to His disciples:

"I will give unto thee the keys of the kingdom of heaven: and whatsoever thou shalt bind on earth shall be bound in heaven: and whatsoever thou shalt loose on earth shall be loosed in heaven." Matt. 16:19.

Last night a dear sister of the church called to tell us that her husband had just returned from the railway office a short time before, violently ill, in an agony of suffering. She was weeping and said, "Mr. Lake, something must be done." How the mind wanders after that something. I said, "Dear Sister, *something* will be done if you and I believe God." I told the other members of the family and we bowed our heads. Nobody spoke a word, but we believed God. About half an hour later the telephone bell rang, and she said, "Brother it is wonderful, the agony is absolutely gone. The Lord has abolished it."

One of the scientific discussions that I have been interested in lately, is regarding the power of the eyes to attract to themselves that upon which they look. Get the principle that is behind that. The power of the eyes to attract to themselves that which they behold. One can readily see that behind the eye there is an action; something within our nature that reaches out and takes possession of the thing which the soul admires, and the soul desires. We draw or attract to ourselves that which we behold. "Beholding as in a glass the glory of the Lord, we are changed into the same image." Bless God, are you sinful? Look on Jesus and be saved. Are you sick? Look on Jesus and be healed.

Let me carry your thought back and connect it with the serpent. The serpent was their peculiar enemy. He has been the symbol of the enemy of the race from the very beginning. "That old serpent, the devil, and Satan," is the Scriptural phrase describing him. But the utterness of his defeat, the wonder of the triumph of redemption, is set forth and portrayed in the fact that he, the symbol of darkness, is erected and nailed to the pole. God said, "Come and look at him. Do not be afraid of him. The power of the promise has overcome him." And bless God, whoever looked, lived. They saw the overcome serpent, and the overcoming Christ.

My how the Lord God taught mankind by this wonderful symbolic lesson not to be afraid of the devil. He wrote it down in every soul of the nation that day, that the Almightiness of God brought their enemy into captivity, and no power of darkness should stand before Almighty God. Our difficulty is in the fact that we have become conscious of our sin and sickness, that we are not looking to the Lord with faith and expectation.

It seems to me in this matter of health, the Children of Israel learned a profound lesson. God was preparing to take them across Jordan. The lesson of the utterness of the defeat of the prince of darkness must have been very clear in their consciousness. After they crossed Jordan they trusted God continuously for many hundreds of years, and they had already trusted God for forty years in the wilderness.

A lesson to older Christians. We have been in the way quite a while. God has taught us varied lessons along the way. God had been their Healer through the forty years in the wilderness, but now here at the end of that time, God is confirming their education in faith in order that when they go across the River Jordan into the land of Canaan, they will remain settled in their faith forever.

In the process of assisting them to realize the utterness of Satan's defeat, just a few days before they asked Arad for the privilege of going through Edom, and he refused them, then Israel,

"Vowed a vow unto the Lord, and said, If thou wilt indeed deliver this people in my hand, then I will utterly destroy their cities. And the Lord hearkened to the voice of Israel, and delivered up the Canaanites; and they, utterly destroyed them and their cities."

An utter and total defeat of the enemy. Israel blotted the nation out, took possession of her territory, dwelt in her houses and cultivated her lands. There was no further to go in demonstration of the utterness of defeat of the enemy, and triumph and victory of God's people.

Then right on top of it God brought this symbol of the serpent and put it up before them, to demonstrate in the spiritual the utterness of God's victory over the enemy of man.

I do not know how these truths work out in other souls, but when I saw for the first time by the Word of God that sickness was not the Will of God, but the work of darkness and that it belonged to the kingdom of darkness, and that Jesus Christ said Satan was its author, everything in my nature rose up to defeat the will of the devil.

Now it may be beloved, that you have been tolerating something in your soul that is out of harmony with God. It may not be that you are sick, but you are tolerating something that is out of harmony with God.

The other day I sat by the bedside of a poor fellow who was being utterly consumed of disease. I talked with him a few minutes along the line that Christ came to destroy the works of the devil. As I sat analyzing the brother, I asked, "Brother, where did this difficulty originate?" He replied, "It originated in my disobedience of the laws of God and man." "All right, who is its author? To what kingdom does it belong?" He answered, "It does not take much reasoning to classify it." I said, "If that is true, God has promised its utter annihilation." He plead, "Oh pray for me that the pain will leave." I replied, "No, never! I cannot do it. But I will pray that the living God will utterly blot it out."

Yes, brother, when you came to God with the sin of your burdened heart, the first thing He did was to blot it out, bless God. And He filled your soul with the consciousness and presence of His glory, and ever since He has been endeavoring to reproduce the likeness of the Lord and Saviour Jesus Christ in you.

Chapter XI

THE GRACE OF DIVINE HEALING

An address given at a Convention in
Chicago, Ill., July 26, 1920.

I want to use a familiar text. "The grace of God that bringeth salvation hath appeared to all men." Titus 2:11. There never was a bigger word than the word "Grace." If we undertake to define and analyze its operations, that beautiful term brings the many-sided gospel of Jesus Christ to the heart with a wonderful clearness. The Grace of Jesus Christ is not His demeanor, neither His beautiful gratuitous giving. It is the DIVINE OUTFLOWING OF THE NATURE OF GOD, heavenly, healing loveliness, and holy balm, it comes to the needy world; not only as a sin-saving action of God, but as a healing virtue, stealing into the natures of men, soothing away their pains, changing the very chemicalization of their being, making them whole, and blessing them through salvation, healing and abiding rest in God. Divine healing is no mystery. It is the definite action of the Spirit of God in the souls and the bodies of men.

Grace of God on an Individual

There is a Grace of God that rests on a community. There is a Grace of God that rests upon a church; the Grace of God that rests upon an individual. In South Africa, there used to be an old lady who visited our home once in a while. She was one of the sweetest, most blessed creatures I ever met. My, when she came into my office and sat down for five minutes, she brought the consciousness of God, a restfulness and a peace of mind. From her whole person there seemed to radiate that blessedness that can be described only as the grace of God, and the very atmosphere would become pregnant with it. I would make excuses to take her through the house. I wanted her to leave that beautiful emanation all over the place. Because when she was gone, it seemed the house settled down, the noisy children ceased to influence, and all invisible unrest disappeared. It was the Grace of God.

Tuesday of this week, at Portland, we had an experience with a young woman who was on the way to the river to take her life. Somehow she felt impelled to come up to our healing rooms. She sat for a little while and we talked to her, soothed her heart, and tried to get her to God. I said to those present, "I wish someone could take her and love her for a little while." Soon a lady of our church came in and I introduced her to the poor girl. I said, "Just take her home with you. Put your arms around her and let her feel your love. Let her know what the Grace of God is, not by preaching, but by contact." She took her home and four days later the young woman came back, after having given her heart to God. In the meantime things worked out in her family; she went back home to be a blessing to her brother, her sister and dear old parents and the kingdom of God. This is the same Grace of healing that flowed from the loving Hands and heavenly Spirit of Jesus.

I wonder when the Lord Jesus Christ passed down the highway as He walked from Bethany to Jerusalem, if the atmosphere was not alive, pregnant with the beautiful light of His Divine presence and blessing. And I haven't a bit of doubt that when someone walked down that way after Jesus passed, and they breathed the air that Jesus breathed, that they felt the life of God that was shed from His person, and were healed by the virtue of the fact that Christ had been there. That same healing Grace permeated the atmosphere around dear old Peter, so that the sick were healed as far from him as his eventide shadow reached.

That is my ideal of a Christian heart, a Christian life, a Christian church or a Christian ministry. My soul desires, by the Grace of God, that out through these old brick walls, there will flow that beautiful emanation of Christ throughout old dirty Chicago, that will discover disease in every part of the city, and heal both soul and body. That this Grace may bring to the heart of man made free from sin's power, a life joined to God, a consciousness of holy oneness with our Father God, through Jesus Christ. Atonement makes at-one-ment, in body, soul and spirit with Christ, both in salvation through Him and in ministry for Him.

How blessed it is when once in a while we walk suddenly into the presence of one rich with the light and life of God. As we emerge from the storms of life, as we come out of the turmoil, passing into the presence of the heart that balm and sweetness indicating the presence of God, and leaving upon our life a divine influence that gives us restfulness of mind, restfulness of heart, and sunlit soul, the God-lit life, instantly there comes to the quiet in God.

There is the Grace of God that goes underneath the soul of man, that by the blessed gift of the Spirit, lifts from the life forever the shadows and darkness that sin has brought, and takes away the corrosion that has come upon the soul of man, and by the Grace of God lets the heart of man understand the blessed touch of the Son of God that imparts eternal life. Blessed be His name.

"Down in the human heart, crushed by the tempter,
  Feelings lie buried that Grace can restore.
Touched by a loving heart, wakened by kindness,
  Chords that were broken will vibrate once more."

O yes beloved, there is a Grace of God that goes underneath the life and lifts the nature of man into beautiful holiness and heavenly contact, into the consciousness of purity, the realization of power, blessed be His Name forever.

Curse Removed From a Drunkard

One morning a distress call came from a woman on behalf of her husband. Some other ministers and I responded. We found the man in delirium tremens, begging his wife for just a little more whiskey, and making the usual promises an insane man will make. We knelt by his bed, laid hands upon him, lifted our hearts in love and faith to God. "The grace that bringeth salvation" appeared, stole into that man's soul, and in five minutes his pains were gone, the curse had departed, and he never wanted whiskey again. Later he called on me in Portland, Oregon, took my hands and poured out his tears and love for God, told of his success in life, and all the rest of the beautiful story. The Lord was not in the cyclone, or in the fire, or in the earthquake. He is now as then in the still small voice and the healing touch of Divine gentleness.

Every soul should have its own contact with God. If that touch has not been real to your own heart yet, it may become real. Bless God! Mrs. Graham was dying of pneumonia. As I entered into her home I was met by Brother Fogwill, coming out. He said, "John, you are too late. She is gone." The flames of God came over my heart and though she had not breathed for twenty-three minutes, the breath and the power of Christ came upon her and she is continuing her ministry for God and man.

Beloved the Christian life is a glorious doorway into God, through Jesus Christ, into the divinest secrets that the soul of man ever desired to attain. And bless His Name, you and I tonight are privileged to enter that doorway, and to know Him "whom to know is life eternal."

The Woman in the Coma of Death

Some days past, Dr. McInturff and I were called to the bedside of a woman that was dying. She had gone out of her mind. Had become unconscious, and was then in the coma of death. Her nurse told us that she had not been able to speak, hear, or see for a number of days. We knelt, prayed, and left, with a feeling that God was there, though we could detect no action in the woman's body so far as we could tell. We went away with the consciousness that our prayer was heard, and the work was done.

Weeks passed and there was no report of the woman's condition. Until finally one day the mother-in-law of the woman walked into the office to tell how wonderfully God had healed and delivered the woman. Later the lady herself, walked in, and for an half hour told of the wonderful inner action of the Spirit that went into her life even as we prayed. She said, "Brother, as you knelt by my bedside, I became conscious that someone was there. All I knew was that the sound of the voices was different from others. Then you proceeded to put your hands on my head, and something began to steal down through my brain; the awful torture gradually subsided. After awhile I became still and quiet in my soul. Then a voice began to speak to me about my Lord and Saviour Jesus Christ. It bade me have faith in God, and said that I should come out of this condition, and be a blessing to my home and husband. I have now come to tell you that your prayer was heard." We never spoke of the Grace of salvation, but the living presence of the Spirit came to her and made her to know of "the grace of God that bringeth salvation."

The world is in need of a knowledge of Christ's way of salvation and healing. The whole subject of its actuality has become greatly dimmed in the hearts of men. There is a dire need of a wondrous clarifying of the spiritual atmosphere, in order that His power may be made effective to those who turn their hearts thither-ward. This then is a part of the mission of Pentecost. Not only to declare Christ as a Saviour and a Healer, but to manifest Him by God's Grace in daily life, through God-anointed lives and hands to carry that blessed Grace of God, and transmit it to whosoever will. Put your hands on the sick, believer; Jesus Christ commanded it, and "they shall recover." I am praying that upon your souls there will come the presence of God, through Christ, that will make you realize yourself as a minister of the Lord and Saviour, with a mission from God, and that in His Name you too, my brother and sister, will go forth to carry this light and power to whosoever will.

A young man dying of consumption came to our healing rooms and said, "I am no Christian. I have not been interested in religion. I have heard that people are healed here. I am dying and have no hope. Tell me what you have to say in the shortest words you can." I answered, "Young man, God is able to deliver you. He is able to heal you. He is ready to do it right now." He replied, "I haven't any faith." I said, "But I am a child of God, I am a son of God, and I have faith." And without more ado I proceeded to pray. That man was healed. His sister was converted and healed, and other members of the family were saved. I received word telling of a movement of God in the community, where a dozen people are now seeking God unto salvation.

Chapter XII

THE LAW OF LIFE AND LAW OF DEATH

"There is therefore now no condemnation to them which are in Christ Jesus, who walk not after the flesh, but after the Spirit. For the law of the Spirit of life in Christ Jesus hath made me free from the law of sin and death." Rom. 8:1-2.

There are three laws here. First, there is the *law of the flesh*. Second, there is the *law of death*. Third, "the *law of the Spirit of life in Christ Jesus,* (which) hath made me free from the law of sin and death."

Man is compelled to recognize that there exists a law of death in his own members. The hair turns gray, the eyes grow dim, not because you are sick, but because the law of death is operating in you. Wrinkles come in your face, the body gets old. All these common evidences are noticeable every day, and teach us the operation of the law of death that exists in our members, permeating our being and established in our nature.

The natural consequence is that in spite of all you can do, you will die. You may live as sanitary as you know how, but eventually you will die, for there is a law of death that claims every man in the world. Until this hour, that one unconquerable foe of the race is death.

I heard this amusing incident which illustrates that truth. A lawyer, Gilluly, had been trying a case against a very prominent doctor. Gilluly had secured the names of the doctor's prominent patients who had died. So he appeared in court and among other questions, he asked, "Doctor, you had a patient once by the name of so-and-so. Where is he?" The doctor answered, "He is dead." "Now then you had another patient by the name of so-and-so. Where is he?" "He is dead." Well you can imagine the effect of an attorney keeping that up for half an hour. It looked as though all the patients the doctor had treated had died. And of course if the doctor lived long enough to sign death certificates, he would have to sign them for all the people, as there is a law of death that claims every man.

The Soul and the Law of Death

We see that in the natural order, man will die. But I want to call your attention to this law on the spiritual side. Just exactly as there is a law that claims your body in death, there is a law of death that claims your soul too, unless you do something to counteract it. The law of death will claim your soul as well as your body, in the natural, in spite of everything you can do.

People seem to think that they must be terrible sinners in order to lose their soul. That is not true. All you have to do is to be naturally careless. Just live like cows do. Just like the dogs do. Just live like the horses do. Just be an animal. Dogs are honest, the cows are honest, horses are honest. They do not steal, or lie, or swear, or get drunk.

Suppose you put yourself on the same level with the animals, as men are doing every day. What will be the end of this? Well your body will die, and you will lose your soul too. Not because you have been a highwayman. That is not the reason. Just because you have been so careless that you have not taken pains to come to the Lord Jesus Christ, and secure from Him the only element that will stop that process of death in the soul.

Man Who Lived 152 Years

I saw a slab in Westminister Abbey for a man who had died at the age of 152 years, by the name of Parr. On account of his great age some of the royalty got a hold of him and brought him to London, away from his plain diet and rural life. They wined him and dined him and in a few days it proved too much for him and he died. It does not make any difference if a man lives fifty years, or seventy five years, or one hundred and fifty two years, like Fred Parr did; he will die.

They die because there is a law of death, and this body is doomed to die by that law of death. That law of death came into being through sin, through disobedience to God. Before man sinned there was no death. There were no heavy eyes, no heart breaks, no soul wrenches, no clods rattling on coffin lids. But sin came, and "through sin death entered into the world." Through sin! That is the cause of it. That is the reason death came. Sin generated decay which is sickness, and death which is dissolution.

Antidotes

In nature we have antidotes. I knew of a farmer out in the country, James Sawyer, who came into the house during his wife's absence, and took what he supposed was the medicine that he had been in the habit of using. It sat up on the clock shelf. His wife had carbolic acid on the clock shelf too, and he grabbed the first bottle he saw, and instead of getting the medicine bottle he got the carbolic acid. But before he lost all power of control he crawled down into the cellar, and got a big pail of lard and proceeded to eat it. Every once in a while his stomach would become overloaded and he would vomit. It was a fine case of presence of mind for a farmer in the country, who probably had nothing else available that would have helped him in such a circumstance. It saved his life.

The Divine Antidote

There is an antidote for sin, the deadliest poison, something that will counteract sin and nullify its power. Jesus Christ knew that this condition of sin rested upon

the world. He came by the grace of God to provide
something that would stop its progress, nullify its power,
and give man deliverance from death.

Your soul is dying, dying, dying because of disobedience to God. Because you live in conformity with that
law of death, you are going on dying and dying, and you
will die, unless you put yourself in harmony and contact
with another law.

Nobody can put you in harmony with that other
law. You must do it yourself. No man can put you in
harmony with that law of life, "The law of the Spirit of
life in Christ Jesus." He is its source. It is from His Soul
that it is ministered unto you. It is His Spirit that does it.
So the Apostle rejoiced that he was made "free from
the law of sin and death."

Operation of Fear In the Physical

That law operates in the physical as well as the
spiritual. A man is in a state of fear. Someone has typhoid
fever. They are placarding the houses to keep others from
getting in contact with that dread disease. Now fear
causes your mind to become subjective. When you are full
of fear, your pores will absorb everything around you.
You are drawing into yourself what is around you. That
is the way people absorb disease.

I was ministering one time where the bubonic plague
was raging. You could not hire people for a thousand
dollars to bury the dead. At such times the government
has to take hold of the situation. But I never took the
disease.

Operation of the Law of Life

Now watch the action of the *law of life*. Faith belongs
to the law of life. Faith is the very opposite of fear. Faith
has the opposite effect in spirit, and soul, and body. Faith
causes the spirit of man to become confident. It causes the

mind of man to become restful, and positive. A positive mind repels disease. Consequently, the emanation of the Spirit destroys disease germs.

And because we were in contact with the Spirit of life, I and a little Dutch fellow with me went out and buried many of the people who had died from the bubonic plague. We went into the homes and carried them out, dug the graves and put them in. Sometimes we would put three or four in one grave.

We never took the disease. Why? Because of the knowledge that the law of life in Christ Jesus protects us. That law was working. Because of the fact that a man by the action of his will, puts himself purposely in contact with God, faith takes possession of his heart, and the condition of his nature is changed. Instead of being fearful, he is full of faith. Instead of being absorbent and drawing everything to himself, his spirit repels sickness and disease. The Spirit of Christ Jesus flows through the whole being, and emanates through the hands, the heart, and from every pore of the body.

You observe that we lay hands upon the sick for healing. What for? Simply that the Spirit of life in Christ Jesus that dwells in the Christian may flow through our hands into their body. We were praying for a sick woman last night, when I saw the Spirit of God strike. It flashed through her soul just as consciously as a stroke of lightning. I felt it in my spirit and I know the one we were praying for was conscious of it too. "The law of the spirit of life in Christ Jesus hath made me free from the law of sin and death."

If a man were traveling down the road in a certain direction, and were aware that at the end of that pathway he is going to drop over into the grave, and that not only his body is going into that grave, but he is going to lose his soul, we would naturally think that a sane man would stop. I wonder what keeps a man from exercising good old-fashioned horse sense? Some power somewhere is exercising itself to keep him in that state of mind, so that he acts like a man that is drugged. The soul is asleep. It is in a dormant state. The soul of man is drugged by the devil's power.

No sane man would come to the end of his journey, losing both soul and body, if he realized it. He is not aware. He is not awake. His soul is in a stupor. That is the reason that we preach with all our energy, to arouse men out of that lethargy. The Word of God says, "Awake thou that sleepest, and arise from the dead."

Don't you see that when men turn their faces heavenward and look to the Lord Jesus for salvation, instantly by faith they contact the law of life, and the result is the consciousness of salvation.

In the natural world there is a great law called gravitation. This causes everything to move toward the center of the earth. That is the reason that when you throw anything into the air, it will come down again. There is another law called levitation. It is the powerful operation of that law by which we will rise to meet the Lord in the air.

In Christ Jesus there is a law that lifts you up, just as in the natural there is a law of death that pulls you down. Christianity and salvation are the conscious taking of yourself out of the law of death and putting yourself out of that law of death into the conscious control of the law of life. "The law of the Spirit of life in Christ Jesus hath made me free from the law of sin and death."

I want to leave this written upon your soul by the grace of God. Religion is not a matter of sentiment. It is not the matter of how you feel, or how I feel. It is the matter of the inevitable law, the conscious law, established eternally. In the path of darkness, you will keep going on downward, and death will be the result. Let your heart turn upward, embrace the Lord Jesus Christ, let

His living Spirit get a hold of your soul, and you will be lifted heavenward, just as naturally as can be.

You are in sickness and you are down. It is terrible to look into the faces of some of these woe-begone people. I visited with a dear man today and his soul was in the gloom of darkness. He said, "I can sight something and see further than my eyes can see, and after a while it concentrates into a narrow sphere ten inches in diameter, and it is total blackness. Tell me what is that?" I replied, "Dear Brother, that is due to the fact that there is no life of God and light of heaven in your heart." That poor man was under the law of death.

A man came to me one day and said, "Mr. Lake, I am haunted." I asked, "What do you mean?" He answered, "I have been associated with bad people who I believe were demon-possessed, and it seems when I walk up the street there are a horde of demons around me and I can see them. They grin at me and laugh and taunt me." I replied, "Brother, I will pray for you." I called on God to cast those demons out of his life, to bind them, and send them back to hell, or wherever else they came from. After we prayed he sat up with a sigh of relief, and said, "Brother, I am free." I added, "Brother, you have come out of the regions of darkness and sin and hell, and Christ and the Spirit of God have put you over on His side, under the law of the Spirit of life. You ought to see the angels of God, with as much readiness as you did the demons."

The next day he returned very joyfully, and said, "Before I got to the bank I saw an angel, and there have been angels around me all day. As I walked up the street there was an angel that walked beside me."

Divine Protection

During that great plague that I mentioned, they sent a government ship with supplies and a corps of doctors.

One of the doctors sent for me, and said, "What have you been using to protect yourself? Our corps has this preventative and that, which we use as protection, but we concluded that if a man could stay on the ground as you have and keep ministering to the sick and burying the dead, you must have a secret. What is it?"

I answered, "Brother that is the 'law of the Spirit of life in Christ Jesus.' I believe that just as long as I keep my soul in contact with the living God so that His Spirit is flowing into my soul and body, that no germ will ever attach itself to me, for the Spirit of God will kill it." He asked, "Don't you think that you had better use our preventatives?" I replied, "No, but doctor I think that you would like to experiment with me. If you will go over to one of these dead people and take the foam that comes out of their lungs after death, then put it under the microscope you will see masses of living germs. You will find they are alive until a reasonable time after a man is dead. You can fill my hand with them and I will keep it under the microscope, and instead of these germs remaining alive, they will die instantly." They tried it and found it was true. They questioned, "What is that?" I replied, "That is 'the law of the Spirit of life in Christ Jesus.' When a man's spirit and a man's body are filled with the blessed presence of God, it oozes out of the pores of your flesh and kills the germs."

Suppose on the other hand, my soul had been under the law of death, and I were in fear and darkness? The very opposite would have been the result. The result would have been that my body would have absorbed the germs, these would have generated disease and I would have died.

You who are sick, put yourself in contact with God's law of life. Read His Word with the view of enlightening your heart so that you will be able to look up with more confidence and believe Him. Pray that the Spirit of God will come into your soul, take possession of your body, and its power will make you well. That is the exercise of the law of the Spirit of life in Christ Jesus.

A man came to me about a month ago, and said, "Mr. Lake, I am in awful darkness and dread. If there is a hell, I am in it now." I inquired, "Brother, what put you there?" He shrugged his shoulders. I said, "There is some place where you departed from the law of righteousness, from the place of truth, from the law of life in Christ Jesus, and let the law of death get hold of you."

Then I told him the story of Christian in Pilgrim's Progress. How that Christian lay down, and while he slept his roll, which was the witness of God, fell out of his pocket. He awoke and went on without noticing. But as he went down the road he began to have doubts. He wondered if he had been saved. After a while everything grew blacker, and finally he discovered he had lost his roll. What did he do? Well he said, "I will go back." He turned back, went to the tree where he had been asleep, and found his roll. He got back his witness. "His Spirit beareth witness with our spirit that we are the children of God."

Jesus is the Law of life. Life comes from His soul. He breathes it into your heart. He pulses it into your nature. He transmits it into your body. That is what makes people whole.

Chapter XIII
THE INTEGRITY OF GOD'S PEOPLE

"Back to Christ" is a slogan that is being adopted by real Christians everywhere these days. The result of unbelief being taught in our educational institutions was discussed by W. J. Bryan in a recent sermon. The expression behind Bryan's sermon was "I sent my boy to college a Christian; he returned an atheist." That experience has become so common that it is not a matter of surprise any more. Consequently the world has drifted into the attitude of mind that the individual who believes the truth of God as expressed in His Word is intellectually a back number. He is not an up-to-dater.

The Science of the Gospel

I have taken this ground for many years in debate and otherwise that there is a science of the Gospel of Jesus Christ so profound that no man with a simple knowledge of material science, discovers it or knows anything about it. It is beyond his ken. But through simple faith the souls of men enter into a relationship with God, where God makes known to them in consciousness His Presence, His love, His power, His salvation which is indisputable, for the evidence from heaven is not to be disputed.

When a Christian is truly born of God, and has really received from God witness to that salvation, you cannot cause that individual to doubt or question, if he is living in the light of God. You can bring all the scientific disputations to bear upon him, but they have no weight. That is the reason that the Christian who does not even know the meaning of the word "psychology," or "science" goes through life with a song in his soul and a triumph in his spirit, because he has something in his heart that the other man does not know anything about.

Janitor Healed in the University

I love to tell this incident because it illustrates that splendid truth. I was lecturing at the Medical Department of the University of Dublin, by arrangement of W. T. Stead, and was going down the line of action of the power of God in men's lives in salvation, in healing, in bringing the consciousness of God in clearness to their lives. The janitor and his wife were doing some work in the back of the hall. The old man was a rheumatic cripple. As I went along I said, "Old man come down this way." Then I inquired, "What is the matter with you?" He answered, "It is rheumatism." He told me he had had it for ten years. I prayed for him, asking that the Lord might heal him; as I did so, his dear simple soul went up to God, and the faith of God in my soul went up to God for him, and the old man was healed. I had the consciousness before I ceased praying, that he was healed.

The chairman addressing one of the professors, said "Explain this occurrence." And he proceeded to give a long technical psychological statement. The janitor's wife, in her delight, broke in with "Ach, it's just Jasus."

Night before last I prayed for a man at Carlton, Oregon. He had a slipped vertebra, the result of an accident. He suffered agony. I laid hands on him and prayed, and before I ceased praying I was conscious that he was healed. But he did not know it. By the Spirit of God one is aware of what God has accomplished. So when I finished praying, I put my hand upon his stomach and I said, "Bend down, and do it quickly." The poor fellow was so startled, perspiration came upon his brow, because he expected the usual thing to take place. But God had healed him.

Now get the scientists of earth to define that power that instantly heals, and tell you what and how it is applied. There are some things that the Christian soul learns that nobody else knows anything about.

Once I was talking with Professor James, psychologist of Harvard, a splendid man. We were discussing Harold Bixbee's books, "Twice Born Men," and "Broken Earthenware." He said this pungent thing, "Lake, it is a rather sad thing that when we want to get a good example of what you Christians term real conversion, we are compelled to go over to the slums of London, to the work of the Salvation Army to find it." I replied, "James, my judgment is that it is such fellows as you and all the other big lights, who brought that condition to pass." There was a time when every godly Methodist had the testimony from heaven that he was a son of God, and if he did not have it he was not a Methodist. That was what distinguished Methodism.

The Overcomer

I want to talk to you a little about the overcomers. Job is the best Old Testament example of the real overcomer in the Bible. As I study the Word of God, I see great outstanding types in the Old Testament. Enoch, a type of the translation. Enoch was not aware of what time he was going away. He just travelled so far out in God that he could not get back again. There became a detachment; the earth's environment let go, and the heavenly drew him; Enoch never returned. "And Enoch walked with God: and he was not; for God took him." Gen. 5:24.

Elijah is another type of translation. But Elijah knew he was going. The whole school of the prophets knew it. He went over to Jericho, and when he got to Jericho the prophets there said to Elisha, "Knowest thou that the Lord will take away thy master from thy head to day?" 2 Kings 2:5. Where did they get it? They got it from heaven.

Elisha's Persistence

Oh, there are some fine lessons; here is one of them. Elisha persisted in being with Elijah. Elijah tried to dismiss him several times, but without avail. He answered, "As the Lord liveth, and as thy soul liveth, I will not leave thee." Elijah could not get rid of him, and after they crossed the Jordan on dry ground, Elijah said, "Ask what I shall do for thee, before I be taken from thee." 2 Kings 2:9. Elisha answered: "I pray thee, let a double portion of thy spirit be upon me." Elijah replied, "Thou hast asked a hard thing: nevertheless, if thou see me when I am taken from thee, it shall be so unto thee; but if not, it shall not be so." Vs. 10

So they went on, and as they talked—oh, you dear folk that get your eyes off the Lord and on the phenomena, get this lesson. You hear folk say, "Did you see how the power of God came on that fellow? My didn't the power of God come on him wonderfully when I prayed." And they were so entertained with the power of God that the eyes were taken off the Lord, and they wondered why nothing was accomplished.

"And it came to pass, as they still went on, and talked, that, behold, there appeared a chariot of fire, and horses of fire, and parted them asunder; and Elijah went up by a whirlwind into heaven." Vs. 11.

A flaming chariot and horses rush between them, and they are parted, but Elisha had the good sense to keep his eyes on the prophet. The chariot and horses from heaven, rushing between them, did not have power enough to take Elisha's eyes of Elijah. He was watching and expecting something, and there was nothing going to attract his attention from the object of his desire, not even if it came from heaven. And that test was applied by God Himself. If a chariot and horses broke through the window today, would we forget about the Lord in our interest in the phenomena?

One Cause of Failure

I had a young preacher on whom a marvelous power of the Spirit rested. I was in a meeting once when he prayed for about 150 people, and I think one hundred or more were prostrated as he prayed. I observed that the first twenty five were really healed, and after that they just fell on the floor. I took him home with me, and I inquired, "Tell me why were there only twenty five healed?" He answered, "Well, I do not know. Why do you think that they were not all healed? But weren't those first twenty five wonderful?" I replied, "I examined them; they were not all healed. Now I will tell you what was the matter. When you started to pray for those people, your soul was lost in the Son of God and you were hardly conscious anybody had fallen. But when you saw them strewed all around you, then you forgot the face of Jesus, and became absorbed in the phenomena. That is why they did not get anything. You forgot to connect faith with the power."

Beloved faith is more important than power. Faith commands power and vitalizes it.

Job a Type of the Overcomer

To me Job stands for another class. That is the class of overcomers that has endured the most dreadful testing. Job is the outstanding Old Testament type of the overcomer. He overcame the most dreadful tribulation. It gives one of the finest, behind the scene views, that there is in all the Word of God.

Somewhere where God was, the sons of God gathered before the Lord, apparently to make report, or council, and among them appeared Satan also. (See Job 1.)

"And the Lord said unto Satan, Whence comest thou? Then Satan answered the Lord, and said, From going to and fro in the earth, and from walking up and down in it. And the Lord said unto Satan, Hast thou considered my servant Job, that there is none like him in the earth, a perfect and upright man, one that feareth God, and escheweth evil?" Job 1:7-8.

Here is a fine distinction between God and Satanic character. The only thing that Satan could understand was his own selfishness. He said, "Doth Job fear God for nought? Hast not thou made a hedge about him, and his house, and about all that he hath on every side?" Vss. 9-10.

That old skunk no doubt had been around the hedge a thousand times, and had looked through every crack. He could not even get at a single she-ass. But the Lord answered, "Behold, all that he hath is in thy power; only upon himself put not forth thine hand." Vs. 12.

God knew His servant Job. He knew he could stand the testing. So Job's testing began. The asses were gone, the camels were gone, and to climax it all a servant came with a report that a cyclone had struck the house where his sons and daughters were drinking wine, and all had perished "and I only am escaped alone to tell thee."

But the final climax came when:

"So went Satan forth from the presence of the Lord, and smote Job with sore boils from the sole of his foot unto his crown." Job 2:7.

The news spread of his awful calamity. His friends gathered to help him. He was an upright man. One of the richest men of the East, a prince. He was not just a good man, and a just, but he was a great, influential, wealthy, godly man.

There are friends and friends. Job's comforters were of the negative kind. Let us not be a gloom pot or a tar brush. If you are my friend, and you come to me, you are going to say something with faith in God in it.

When I had my large healing work in Spokane, Washington, where I used to minister to from 100 to 150 people each day, the Lord would let me see everything in a man's soul dozens of times a day. What did He do it for? For me to run and tell somebody else, or to tell the patient? What would be the good of telling him? If you want to get rid of the difficulty, get him to the Lord and get the blood applied. I think the individual who tells any body else or the person himself, unless God signifies it, is a traitor to Almighty God. I never read a single instance in the New Testament where somebody came along and said, "Brother Paul, tell me what is the matter with me," or "Brother Peter, tell me what is the matter with me." That is the business of the Holy Spirit.

Job's Friends

Job's friends came, and they were wonderful men. You read the addresses of these four men, as they were given to Job, and you will see that they were unsurpassed in Biblical history. But they reasoned from the point of view that calamity cannot come upon the righteous; that it does not belong to the righteous. The burden of their words was, "Job you have sinned. There is no question about it, you have sinned."

Job's friends tried to convince him of sin, that some secret sin had come into his life, but they failed. He said it was not so. He got terribly discouraged and awfully confused; he could not understand why this calamity had come upon him, but he held fast his integrity before God.

Beloved, that is one of the strongest weapons that the devil has. I sought God for the Holy Ghost for nine months. I crawled on my face, and watered my way with tears, and the devil almost whipped me out on this proposition. Every time I got close to God where I ought to have been baptized, I would see every miserable old sin I ever committed in all my life, until my soul would become discouraged, and I said to myself, "Why, God can never baptize me in the Holy Ghost. I am too sinful." In that, I disregarded the Blood of Jesus Christ, that had covered my sin and blotted out my transgressions long before.

These men loved Job. They came to him when he

was lying on the ash heap, scraping himself with a piece of pottery; they sat there seven days and nights and never said a word. They were waiting for a solution. Their soul was seeking a reason. Eventually they spoke when they believed they had found a reason. But they were mistaken.

One of the beautiful points in the record of Job, was at the time he was just pouring out his soul, even cursing the day in which he was born. God gave him a beautiful revelation. (Notice that he never cursed God. No, not a word, not an utterance that would indicate lack of faith in God.) Oh, God was helping him there to overcome. Job says,

"For I know that my Redeemer liveth, and that he shall stand at the latter day upon the earth: And though after my skin worms destroy this body, yet in my flesh shall I see God: Whom I shall see for myself, and mine eyes shall behold, and not another; though my reins be consumed within me." Job 19:25-27.

He would know Him; they were familiar friends.

God Answers Job

Eventually God Himself comes. The whirlwind announces His appearing, and the Lord begins to talk to Job, and down through four chapters God Almighty talks to Job. He says: "Who is this that darkeneth counsel by words without knowledge? Gird up now thy loins like a man; for I will demand thee, and answer thou me . . ." Job 38:2-7.

And the Lord goes down the line on poor old Job for four chapters. O my, after he had listened to the Lord for a while, Job comes through with a confession. He said, "Wherefore I abhor myself, and repent in dust and ashes." Job 42:2-6.

God was too big for him. He had not comprehended Him; His way and His purpose were too large for Job's

understanding. Beloved isn't that our difficulty? When
you go around the world and see some Christians, you
find they are trying to bring God down to their own
measure. I knew about a dozen and a half saints who just
coralled the Kingdom of God, and nobody would ever
get into the kingdom excepting those associated with that
dozen and a half. One night as I was visiting them, I
thought, "If the Lord had you on His Hands, He would
have trouble forevermore." They had become so con-
tracted in their spirit, it was no bigger than a chicken's.
That is not the Spirit of Jesus Christ. The peculiar charm
of the Son of God was that He was absolutely universal.
Broad as the sunlight, blessing every man, Saviour for the
whole world.

Come with your sins of ignorance as Job, come with
your sickness. Let the whole world come with its sins,
and the Blood of Jesus will blot them out.

I visited an old German lady on one occasion. She
was wonderfully anointed of God some years past. God
gave her a great ministry of healing. The governor of
the state had a dying sister; they brought the dying sister
to the dear old lady and she was instantly healed. Then
Mayor B........ took his dying sister-in-law to her, and she
was healed. Others were instantly healed. After awhile
she got so jealous for the glory of God, she refused to
pray for anybody for fear they would not give the glory
to God.

Beloved, you let the Lord look out for His own glory.
If you have His love and Spirit in your heart, flood it out
on somebody and take a chance on the Lord getting the
glory. He will get the glory all right when the soul is
redeemed and healed.

So the Lord encouraged Job to forget himself, and
pray for his friends, and as he did so, the Lord turned
his captivity into a blessing. The Lord restored his body,
and gave him twice as many possessions as he had in
the beginning.

Chapter XIV
THESE SIGNS SHALL FOLLOW

Jesus said, "These signs shall follow them that believe." Not the doubter, but them that believe in the Name, the Name of Jesus. "They shall cast out devils; they shall speak with new tongues; they shall take up serpents; and if they drink any deadly thing, it shall not hurt them; they shall lay hands on the sick and they shall recover." Someone asks: "What does it mean to cast out devils?" It means that the man with the Holy Ghost dwelling in him is the master, and has dominion over every devilish force and counterfeit. At Johannesburg, some said: "Your power is hypnotism." One night God demonstrated through us the falsity of that accusation. The power that is within the true Christian is the power of the Living Christ, and "Greater is he that is within you, than he that is in the world." 1 John 4:4.

I can best illustrate by introducing an incident in my own personal ministry.

The Power of God Against Hypnotism

In Johannesburg Tabernacle, at a Sunday service about a year ago, God instantly healed a lame girl. She came from Germiston. She had been suffering for three and a half years from what doctors said was either an extreme case of rheumatism, or the first stage of hip disease. She was not able to get up the steps without assistance, when she came to the platform to be prayed for. They asked her: "How long have you been sick?" She said, "For three and a half years." "Have the doctors treated you?" "Yes; for two and a half years, and then they gave me up." "Who has been treating you for the last year?" "A hypnotist."

Just then a well-known hypnotist arose in the audience, moved forward and took a front seat. The leader said, "Never mind the hypnotist, Jesus is going to heal you right now. In two minutes you will be well." They laid hands on her and prayed, and instantly the Lord delivered her, and she walked up and down the platform several times to demonstrate to herself and the audience that she was well.

I stepped back and looked at her, my heart going out in praise to God for His mercy, when suddenly the Spirit of the Lord descended upon me in power, not in any gentle influence, but with a mighty intense power, a spirit of revulsion against the spirit of the hypnotist. I stepped on the platform directly in front of him and said, "Are you the man who has been hypnotizing this woman?" He replied, "Yes, I am." He rose to his feet and looked toward me in a challenging attitude. I said to him, "In the Name of Jesus Christ, you will never hypnotize anybody again." And before I realized what I was doing, I reached over the front of the platform, grasped his collar with my left hand, while with my right I slapped him on the back, saying "In the Name of Jesus Christ, the Son of God, you come out of him." He laughed at me and said, "Do you mean to tell me that I cannot hypnotize anybody?" I said, "Yes, sir, that is the end of that thing. The devil that caused you to hypnotize people is out."

He worked all night in an endeavor to hypnotize some subjects, and in the morning at six came to my house saying, "This is a mighty serious business, mister, this is my bread and butter." He wanted me to give him back the power to hypnotize. I explained to him that it was not I but Jesus who cast out the devil. I added, "Brother, it looks to me as if the Lord wanted you to earn an honest living."

He cancelled his engagement at the theater where he was billed to give exhibitions, and the last heard of he was working in a mine and earning an honest living. That demonstrated that there is a mighty manifestation of the Spirit of God that has dominion over every other power. It is still true that in His Name we shall cast out devils.

They Shall Take Up Serpents

This afternoon I heard a brother ask, "What about 'they shall take up serpents'?" Let me tell you a story. Brother Fisher of Los Angeles, California, told me this incident in his own life. He was a Baptist minister at Glendale, a suburb of Los Angeles. He is now associated with Brother George B. Studd in "The Upper Room Mission."

Brother Fisher said, "One morning my wife called me up on the telephone and said the water pipe beneath the house was broken. I went home about ten in the morning. I opened the little door in the basement of the house and on putting my hand in to feel for the pipe, I was bitten by a serpent. At once I commenced to swell. The poison worked into my body fast. What was I to do? I said, 'God, your Word says, "They shall take up serpents." I trust you for this and you must heal me or I'll die.' That afternoon and evening my sufferings were terrible. By midnight my blood was so congealed I was well nigh insensible. Oh, I shall never forget that sense of death creeping over me, steadily, surely until three in the morning. I could pray no more. I ceased to struggle, I fell to the floor; and that instant God healed me. The life of God thrilled through my body, and I was healed." It is true, "They shall take up serpents."

If They Drink Any Deadly Thing It Shall Not Hurt Them

You ask, what about, "If they drink any deadly thing, it shall not hurt them?"

History abounds in instances wherein the early Christians were compelled to drink the juice of the deadly hemlock; but through faith in Jesus one of the deadliest of poisons became harmless as water. According to your faith be it unto you. My own sister's son, Fred Moffat, when a child, entered his father's workshop, and ate some paris green. My sister and brother-in-law sent for me. I quoted the words of our Saviour, "And if they drink any deadly thing, it shall not hurt them." Upon this precious promise of God we rested and Jesus healed the child.

In spite of the clear, convincing testimony of the Scriptures, and the ever accumulating cloud of witnesses, who testify of healing received through faith in Jesus, many preachers and teachers are still blindly rejecting the truth to their own final discomfiture and undoing.

Divine healing is the seal of God's acknowledgment, the proof to the world that Jesus Christ is the Son of God. John the Baptist was in prison. He was troubled with doubt, as to whether Jesus was the Christ. He sent two of his disciples to Jesus to put the question, "Art thou he that should come, or look we for another?" His answer was to appeal to the signs of his ministry. These were, and still are God's answer to doubt and unbelief: "Go and show John again those things which ye do hear and see, The blind receive their sight, the lame walk, and the lepers are cleansed, and the deaf hear, the dead are raised up, and the poor have the Gospel preached to them. And blessed is he whosoever shall not be offended in me." Matt. 11:3-6.

These are still God's seal and endorsement of the preaching of the true Gospel. The preaching that lacks the signs which Jesus promised lacks Divine attestation, by which God confirms the preaching of His own true Gospel. The results now as then should be, "And they went forth and preached everywhere, the Lord working with them and confirming the word with the signs following." Mark 16:20.

Chapter XV

LAKE'S REPLY TO FOUR QUESTIONS CONCERNING HEALING

The Southern Association of Evangelists, who recently met at Hot Springs, Arkansas, in a convention, wrote as follows:

"Rev. John G. Lake,
Spokane, Wash.
Dear Sir:

We are submitting the following questions to about twenty-five leading professors, preachers, and evangelists, for reply, and recognizing your extensive experience in the ministry of healing, trust that you will favor us with an early reply.

The questions are as follows:
FIRST: IS GOD ABLE TO HEAL?
SECOND: DOES GOD EVER HEAL?
THIRD: DOES GOD ALWAYS HEAL?
FOURTH: DOES GOD USE MEANS IN HEALING?"

MY REPLY
Question I. Is God Able to Heal?

Coming as an inquiry from the Church of Christ in her varied branches, as represented by your association, which includes ministers and evangelists of almost every known sect, is a confession of how far the Modern Church has drifted in her faith from that of the Primitive Church of the first four centuries.

That this apostasy is true, may readily be seen by a study of the New Testament, together with the writings of the Christian fathers of the first centuries. That Jesus Himself healed *All* who came to Him; that the apostles after His resurrection and after the outpouring of the

Spirit upon the Church on the day of Pentecost, continued to do the same, is a New Testament fact. It is well known that the Church fathers testified to the vast extent of the miracle-working power of Christ through His followers, until the day of Constantine.

With the establishment of Christianity as the state religion under Constantine, a flood of heathenism poured into the Church, and the vitality of the faith in Christ as Saviour and Healer disappeared. Hordes of unbelievers came into the Church with very slight knowledge of Christ, bringing with them many heathen customs and practices, some of which quickly predominated in the Church. Among these was trust in MAN rather than *Christ*, as healer of the body.

That isolated saints of God and groups of Christians have trusted God exclusively, and proved Him the Healer, is found in the experience of the Church in every century. Among those in modern times were the Hugenots of France, who excelled in their faith in God. Many of them were consciously baptized in the Holy Ghost, and history records that many of them spoke in tongues by the power of the Holy Spirit. The sick were healed through faith in Jesus Christ and the laying on of hands. Many prophesied in the Spirit.

The Waldenses of Europe knew Christ as their Healer, and recorded many instances of wonderful healings.

The Coming of the Reformation

With the coming of Protestantism, and the establishment of the great churches of the present day, little knowledge of Christ as the Healer existed. Protestantism was established on one great principle, the revelation of Martin Luther, his watchword and slogan "The just shall live by faith." Not by works of penance, but through faith in the living, risen, glorified Son of God.

Isolated cases of healing are recorded by Luther, John

Knox, Calvin, and Zewengle, and others of the reformers. With the birth of Methodism, under John Wesley, a fresh impetus was given to the teaching of healing through faith in Jesus. Wesley recorded in his journal, many instances of wonderful healings of the sick, of casting out of demons, and remarkable answers to prayer.

Healing In Modern Times

The modern teaching of healing received a new impetus through Dorothy Trudell, a factory worker in one of the German provinces. Under her ministry many were healed, so that eventually the German Government was compelled to recognize her healing institution at Mennendorf and license it. During the present century a great number of men definitely taught and practiced the ministry of Divine Healing. Among the writers on the subject of healing who are well known to the Christian Church, are A. J. Gordon, Dr. A. B. Simpson, and Rev. Andrew Murray of South Africa.

Andrew Murray's Experience

The Rev. Andrew Murray's experience in healing was as follows: He was pronounced incurable of a throat disease, known as "Preacher's Throat," by many London specialists. In despair he visited the Bethsan Divine Healing Mission in London, conducted by Dr. Bagster. He knelt at the altar, was prayed for by the elders, and was healed. He returned to South Africa, wrote and published a book on Divine Healing, which was extensively circulated in the Dutch Reform Church of South Africa, of which he was the recognized leading pastor. The effect of the book was to call the people's attention to the fact that Jesus is the Healer still. Great celebrations took place in the various churches of South Africa when Andrew Murray returned a living example of Christ's power and willingness to heal.

In a short time persons who read of his ministry of healing made request of their pastors to be prayed for, that they might be healed. In some instances the pastors confessed that they had no faith, and could not honestly pray with them for healing. Others made one excuse or another. Eventually the people began to inquire what was the trouble with their pastors. Andrew Murray, the chief pastor had been healed. He had written a book on healing. Members of the Church throughout the land were praying through to God, and finding Him their Healer still. But the preachers in general were confessing lack of faith. So the circulation of the book became an embarrassment to them. Instead of humbly confessing their need to God, and calling upon Him for that measure of the Spirit's presence and power that would make prayer for the sick answerable, they decided to demand the withdrawal of Andrew Murray's book from circulation in the Church, and this was done. Although the truth of the teaching of Divine Healing, and the personal experience in the healing of Andrew Murray, and hundreds of others through his ministry and the ministry of believers in the Church remained unchallenged, Rev. Andrew Murray was requested not to practice the teaching of Divine Healing in the Dutch Reform Church of South Africa.

This experience illustrates with clearness, the difficulties surrounding the introduction of a more vital faith in the living God in the Modern Church. Every Church has had, in a greater or lesser degree, a somewhat similar experience. The usual custom in the Modern Church is that when a preacher breaks out in a living faith and begins to get extraordinary answers to prayer, he is cautioned by the worldy wise, and if persistent, is eventually made to feel that he is regarded as strange. If he still persists, he is ostracized and actually dismissed by some churches and conferences.

Experiences like the above are entirely due to the

failure of the Modern Church to recognize the varied ministries of the Spirit set forth in the New Testament. The Word in the 12th of Corinthians says concerning the order of ministers in the Church that: "God hath set some in the church, first apostles, secondarily prophets, thirdly teachers, and after that miracles, then gifts of healing, helps, governments, diversities of tongues." Thus a ministry for every man called of God is provided. No one conflicting with the other. All recognized as equally necessary to the well-rounded body of Christ.

The Modern Church must come to a realization of other ministries in the Church beside preaching. In the Modern Church the preacher is the soul and center and circumference of his church. The Primitive Church was a structure of faith composed of men and women, each qualifying in his or her particular ministry. One ministered in the healing of the sick, another a worker of miracles, another a teacher of the ways and the will of God, another an evangelist, another a pastor, another an overseer.

It should be an easy matter for any modern Church to adapt itself to the gifts of the Spirit and so remove forever the difficulty that befell the Dutch Reform Church in South Africa, and has befallen our own churches. Instead of discouraging a ministry of the Spirit through the practice of varied gifts in the Church, these ministries and powers may be conserved and utilized for the upbuilding of the kingdom.

The Church at Spokane

A little over five years ago, we established in Spokane, Divine Healing Rooms with a competent staff of ministers. They believed in the Lord as the present, perfect Healer, and ministered the Spirit of God to the sick through prayer and the laying on of hands. The records show that we ministered up to 200 persons a day; that of these, 176 were non-church members. The knowledge of and faith in Jesus Christ as the Healer, has gripped the world outside of the present Church societies, and the numbers of those who believe are increasing with such rapidity that in a short time they may become a majority in many communities.

Question II. Does God Ever Heal?

The New Testament records forty-one cases of healing by Jesus, Himself. In nine of these instances not only were the individuals healed, but multitudes, and in three instances it especially says "great multitudes."

With the growth of His life's work, the demand for extension was imperative, and in Luke 9, we read: "Jesus called his twelve disciples together, and gave them power and authority over all devils, and to cure diseases, and he sent them to preach the kingdom of God and to heal the sick."

When they in turn were overwhelmed with work we read in Luke 10, that Jesus appointed Seventy others also, and sent them into the cities round about, saying, "Heal the sick that are therein, and say unto them, The kingdom of God is come nigh unto you."

If there were any foundation whatever for the foolish belief that only Jesus and the apostles healed, the appointment of these Seventy should settle it. When the Seventy returned from their first evangelistic tour, they rejoiced saying, "Master, even the demons were subject to thy name."

In addition to the Seventy we read that the disciples complained to Jesus, saying: "We saw one casting out devils in thy name; and we forbad him, because he followeth not with us." And Jesus replied, "Forbid him not: for no man shall do a miracle in my name, that can lightly speak evil of me. He that is not against us is for us."

This then makes a New Testament record of eighty-four persons who healed during the life-time of Jesus. Jesus, the twelve apostles, seventy others, and the man who "followeth not with us."

Paul and Barnabas were not apostles during the life-time of Jesus, but we read in the Acts, of their healing many. Paul himself was healed through the ministry of Ananias, an aged disciple, who was sent to him through a vision from the Lord.

Philip was one of the evangelists who preached at Samaria, and under his ministry there were remarkable signs and wonders.

Under the ministry of the Apostle Paul, the sick were not only healed, and the dead raised, but handkerchiefs were brought to the apostle, that they might contact his person. When laid upon the sick, the disease disappeared, and the "demons" departed from them.

The Book of James gives final and positive instructions of what to do in case of sickness. Commanding that if sick, one shall send for the elders of the Church. Concerning their prayer of faith the Word says: "The prayer of faith shall save the sick, and the Lord shall raise him up; and if he have committed sins they shall be forgiven him."

The great number of medieval miracles, deserve respectful treatment and the cumulative evidence of so much concurrent testimony by distinguished and upright men makes it impossible to think that they were all deluded and mistaken.

Ministry of Dr. John Alexander Dowie

During the life of John Alexander Dowie, and before his mentality was affected through overwork, he established a city in the state of Illinois, forty miles north of Chicago, on the lake shore, known as Zion City. This city was established in 1901. In twelve months it had a population of 4000. In three years the population was estimated at ten thousand. The city Council passed by-laws banishing drugs, medicines, and the use of swine's flesh. None of these are used by his followers if they wish to remain in good standing. Their vital statistics reveal their death rate is lower than that of other cities of the same population. Insurance companies were afraid to insure the Zion people because of the well- known fact that they would not employ physicians or medicines. But at present, insurance companies are seeking their business. They are recognized to be among the healthiest people in the United States.

On an occasion at the Chicago Auditorium, persons from all parts of the world who had been healed through his ministry, were invited to send testimonies on a card 2½ X 4½ inches. It required five bushel baskets to hold these cards. They numbered sixty thousand. Ten thousand in the audience rose to their feet testifying to their own personal healing by the power of God, making a grand total of seventy thousand testimonies.

In South Africa, Divine Healing holds such sway among both black and white, that army officers estimated that in the recent war, twenty out of every hundred refused medical aid, and trusted God only. This necessitated in the army the establishment of a Divine Healing Corps, which ministered healing by the Spirit of God.

By the most careful estimates the Church at Spokane reports 100,000 healings in the past five years. Spokane has become celebrated as the greatest Divine Healing center in the world.

Among prominent physicians who have not only been healed of God, but have adopted the ministry of healing through faith in the Lord Jesus Christ are: Phineas D. Yoakum of Los Angeles, head of the Pisgah Institution, whose blessed ministry of healing is recognized by Christians everywhere. Dr. William T. Gentry, of Chicago, who was not only prominent in his profession as a physician, but as the author of Materia Medica in twenty volumes, to be found in every first-class medical library. His publisher sold over 100,000 copies of this work.

To this I add my personal testimony, after twenty-five years in the ministry of healing, that hundreds of thousands of sick have been healed of the Lord, during this period, through churches and missionary societies founded on the pattern of the Primitive Church, finding God's equipment of power from on high.

With this weight of testimony before us, it seems childish to continue debating the ability or willingness of God to heal the sick. Let us rather with open minds and heart receive the Lord Jesus Christ, as Saviour and Healer, and trust Him with our bodies as we trust Him with our souls.

Question III. Does God Always Heal?

In considering the subject of Divine Healing and its applicability to present day needs, the question, "Does God Always Heal?" is uppermost. The Church at large has taught that healing is dependent on the exercise of the Will of God, and that the proper attitude for the Christian to assume is, "If it be thy will." Continuously we hear men say, "No doubt God can heal; He has the power, and He can heal if He will."

We believe that this attitude of mind and this character of reasoning is due to the ignorance of the plain Word and Will of God, as revealed through Jesus Christ. We contend that God is always the Healer. We contend further that it is not necessary for God to will the healing or non-healing of any individual. In His desire to bless mankind, He willed once and for all and forever that man should be blessed and healed. He gave Jesus Christ as a Gift to the world, that this blessing might be demonstrated and His willingness and desire to heal forever made clear.

Christians readily admit that Jesus is the entire expression of the Law and the Life and the Will of God. As such, He demonstrated forever by His words and acts, what the mind of God toward the world is. He healed all who came to Him, never refusing a single individual, but ever bestowed the desired blessing. In healing all and never refusing one, He demonstrated forever the willingness of God to heal all. He healed because it was the nature of God to heal, not because it was a caprice of the mind of God, or because the mind of God was changed toward the individual through some special supplication. Whosoever was ready and willing to receive healing received it from the Lord. His grief in one instance is expressed in the Gospel narrative in that, "He could do there (in Nazareth) no mighty works because of their unbelief, save that he healed a few sick folk."

Men have assumed that it is necessary to persuade God to heal them. This we deny with all emphasis. God has manifested through Christ, His desire to bless mankind. His method of saving the world, and what constitutes His salvation, is shown in Matt. 4:23: "Jesus went about all Galilee, teaching in their synagogues, (revealing the Will of God) and preaching the gospel of the kingdom, and healing all manner of sickness and all manner of disease among the people."

The Parallel of the Dynamo

The method by which men receive the healing power is parallel to the method by which we light our homes through the use of electricity. A dynamo is set up. Through its motion, it attracts to itself the quality known as electricity. Having attracted electricity, it is then distributed through the wires wherever man wills and our homes are lighted thereby. The dynamo did not make the electricity. It existed from time immemorial. It was the discovery of the ability to control electricity that made the lighting of our homes a possibility. Without it, we would still be living by the light of a tallow candle or a kerosene lamp.

In the spiritual world, the spirit of man is the dynamo. It is set in motion by prayer, the desire of the heart. Prayer is a veritable Holy Spirit controlling dynamo, attracting to itself the Spirit of God. The Spirit of God being received into the spirit of man through prayer, is distributed by the action of the will wherever desired. The Spirit of God flowed through the hands of Jesus to the ones who were sick, and healed them. It flowed from His soul, wirelessly, to the suffering ones and healed them also.

The Holy Spirit is thus shown to be the universal presence of God, God omnipresent. The Spirit of God is given to man for his blessing, and is to be utilized by him to fulfill the Will of God.

The Will of God to save a man is undisputed by intelligent Christians. The Will of God to heal every man is equally God's purpose. God has not only made provision that through the Spirit of God received into our lives, our souls may be blessed and our bodies healed, but further, we in turn are expected and commanded by Jesus to distribute the Spirit's power to others, that they likewise may be healed and blessed.

The Spirit of God is ours to embrace. It is ours to apply to the need of either soul or body. Through Christ's crucifixion and through His victory over the grave, Jesus secured from the Father the privilege of shedding the Holy Spirit abroad over the world. This was the crowning climax of the redemptive power of God ministered through Jesus Christ to the world. And from that day to this, every soul is entitled to embrace to himself this blessed Spirit of God, which Jesus regarded so valuable to mankind, so necessary to their health and salvation, that He gave His life to obtain it.

Consequently it is not a question, "Does God always heal?" That is childish. It is rather a question, "Are we willing to embrace His healing?" If so, it is for us to receive. More than this it is for all the world to receive, for every man to receive, who will put his nature in contact with God through opening his heart to the Lord. Jesus knowing the world's need of healing, provided definitely for physicians (disciples, ministers, elders, those with the Gifts of Healing) who would minister, not pills and potions, but the power of God. The Gifts of Healing is one of the nine Gifts of the Spirit provided for and perpetuated forever in the Church. I Cor 12:8-11. The Word says: "Jesus Christ the same yesterday, and today, and forever." Consequently there is healing from every disease, for every man who will in faith embrace the Spirit of God, promised by the Father, and ministered through Jesus Christ, to the souls and bodies of all who desire the blessing.

Peter in his exposition of this fact, says, "By whose stripes ye were healed." The use of "were" in this text indicates that the healing was accomplished in the mind of God when Jesus Christ gave Himself as the eternal Sacrifice, and has never had to be done over again for the healing of any individual. He willed it once; it is done forever. It is yours to have, yours to enjoy, and yours to impart to others.

Question IV. Does God Use Means In Healing?

By the term "means" is understood the varied reme- dies, medicines and potions commonly used by the world at large and prescribed for the sick—in short, Materia Medica. This should be an extremely easy question for anyone to decide. The world has always had her systems of healing. There were one thousand and one systems of healing evolved in all the centuries. They were mankind's endeavor to alleviate suffering. They existed in the days of Jesus, just as they exist today. The ancient Egyptians used them and were as proficient in the practice as our modern physicians. Indeed their knowledge of chemistry in some respects seems to have superseded ours, as they were able to produce an embalming substance that preserved the human body and kept it from dissolution.

The public commonly believes that medicine is a great science, and that its practice is entirely scientific. Whereas, so great a man as Professor Douglas McGlaggen, who occupied the chair of Medical Jurisprudence in the University of Edinborough, Scotland, declared: "There is no such thing as the science of medicine. From the days of Hippocrates and Galen until now we have been stumbling in the dark, from diagnosis to diagnosis, from treatment to treatment."

Dr. John B. Murphy, the greatest surgeon our country has ever produced, has spoken his mind concerning surgery as follows: "Surgery is a confession of helplessness. Being unable to assist the diseased organ, we remove it. If I had my life to live over again, I would endeavor to discover preventative medicine, in hope of saving the organ instead of destroying it."

Just prior to his death he wrote an article entitled "The Slaughter of the Innocents," condemning cutting out of tonsils and adenoids, demonstrating that the presence of inflammation and pus and the consequent enlargement was due to a secretion in the system that found lodgment in the tonsils and that the removal of the tonsils in no way remedied the difficulty, the poison being generated in the system. He purposed to give his knowledge to the public for its protection from useless operations that he regarded criminal.

God's Contrast to Man's Way

What then, did Jesus have in mind as better than the

world's system of healing, which He never used or countenanced? God's remedy is a Person and not a thing. The remedy that Jesus ministered the sick was a spiritual one. It was the Holy Spirit of God. The tangible, living quality and nature of the living God, ministered through the Soul and Hands of Jesus Christ to the sick one.

So conscious was the woman who was healed of the issue of blood, that she had received the remedy, and of its effect and power in her, upon only touching the hem of His garment, that she "felt in her body that she was made whole of that plague." Jesus likewise was aware of the transmission of the healing power, for He said, "Someone hath touched me, for I perceive virtue has gone out of me."

That same virtue was ministered through the hands of the apostles and of the Seventy. It was also ministered by the early Christians, when they received from God, through the Holy Ghost, the ability to minister the Spirit of God to others. Of the twelve apostles it is said: "He gave them power and authority over all devils, and to cure diseases. And He sent them to preach the kingdom of God, and to heal the sick." Luke 9:1-2.

Of the Seventy it is written, "He sent them two and two, before his face into every city and place, whither he himself would come, and said unto them, . . . 'HEAL THE SICK THAT ARE THEREIN, and say unto them, the kingdom of God is come nigh unto you.' "

So vital was this living Spirit of God and its healing virtue in the lives of the early Christians, that it is recorded of Paul that they brought handkerchiefs and aprons to him, that they might touch his body, and when these were laid upon the sick they were healed and the demons went out of them. Acts 19. In this instance even inanimate objects, handkerchiefs and aprons, were receptacles for the Spirit of God, imparted to them from the person of the Apostle Paul.

This was not an experience for the early Christian alone, but is the common experience of men and women everywhere who have dared to disbelieve the devil's lie, so carefully fostered and proclaimed by the church at large, that the days of miracles are past.

Every advanced Christian, who has gone out into God, who has felt the thrill of His Spirit, who has dared to believe that the Son of God lives by the Spirit in his life today, just as He lived in the lives of the early Christians, has found the same pregnant power of God in himself. Upon laying his hands in faith upon others who are sick, he has seen with his own eyes the healing of the sick take place, and realized the transmission of Divine Virtue. Today millions of men and women trust God only, for the healing of their body from every character and form of disease.

What, then, is this means of healing that Jesus gave as a divine gift to Christianity, forever? It is the living Holy Spirit of God, ministered by Jesus Christ to the Christian soul, transmitted by the Christian because of his faith in the Word of Jesus, through his soul and his hands to the one who is sick. This reveals the law of contact in the mind of Jesus when He gave the commandment: "They shall lay hands on the sick, and they SHALL recover." Mark 16:18.

With praise to God we record to His glory, that through twenty-five years in this ministry we have seen hundreds of thousands of persons in many parts of the world, healed by the power of God. Throughout these twenty-five years, in different lands, we have established churches and societies composed of Christian men and women who know no remedy but the one Divine Remedy, the Lord Jesus Christ. They have faith in His redemption and in the presence and power of the Spirit of Christ to destroy sin and sickness in the lives of men forever.

In our own city, for five years, no day has passed in

which we have not seen the healing of many. For five years we have ministered, with our associate pastors, in The Church at Spokane alone, to an average of from one hundred and fifty to two hundred sick per day, who come from all quarters of the land, and even from foreign countries, to receive the healing power of God. These healings have included almost every known form of disease.

The majority of these healings have been of persons pronounced hopeless by their physicians. Many of them had spent their all, some tens of thousands of dollars, for doctors, medicines, and operations. They found the Lord Jesus Christ, and the ministry of healing by the power of God, just as efficacious today as it ever was, thereby demonstrating the truth of the Word of God.

Christ For The Nations
International Missions

Literature Program

International Bible Schools

Support to Orphans

Native Church Program

Humanitarian Aid & World Relief

CHRIST FOR THE NATIONS
P.O. Box 769000 • Dallas, TX 75376-9000
1-800-933-2364 • www.cfni.org